Remote Yet United: Organizational Design for Hybrid and Fully Remote Teams

J.P. Greyson

Copyright© 2023 J.P. Greyson

All rights reserved.

ISBN: 9798393850098

Introduction

The world of work has undergone a significant transformation in recent years. With the increasing adoption of remote and hybrid work models, organizations must adapt their structures and strategies to optimize performance and maintain employee engagement. This e-book will guide you through the key principles of organizational design, providing valuable insights, practical tools, step-by-step guides, and real-life examples to help you create an effective and inclusive organizational structure for hybrid and fully remote teams.

Table of Contents

Introduction 1

Chapter 1: Understanding Hybrid and Fully Remote Teams 4

    1.1. Defining Hybrid and Remote Work Models 5

    1.2. Benefits and Challenges 9

    1.3. Key Factors Influencing Organizational Design 12

Chapter 2: Designing an Effective Organizational Structure 15

    2.1. Traditional vs. Agile Organizational Structures: In-depth Comparison and Considerations for Remote Work 16

    2.2: Principles of Organizational Design for Hybrid and Fully Remote Teams 22

    2.3: Implementing a Remote-Friendly Organizational Structure 27

Chapter 3: Communication and Collaboration 32

    3.1: Building a Communication Framework 32

    3.2: Leveraging Technology for Effective Collaboration 37

    3.3: Encouraging a Culture of Openness and Transparency . 41

Chapter 4: Performance Management in Hybrid and Remote Teams 46

    4.1: Setting Clear Expectations and Goals 48

    4.2 Monitoring and Measuring Performance 53

    4.3: Feedback and Performance Reviews 57

Chapter 5: Employee Engagement and Well-being – Introduction 62

    5.1: Fostering a Sense of Belonging 64

    5.2: Encouraging Work-Life Balance 69

    5.3: Supporting Mental Health and Well-being 74

Chapter 6: Real-Life Examples of Successful Hybrid and Remote Organizations 79

    6.1: GitLab: Embracing Transparency and Async Communication 81

    6.2: Buffer - Building a Culture of Trust and Flexibility 86

    6.3: Automattic: Decentralizing Decision-Making 90

Chapter 7: Implementing Change: A Step-by-Step Guide 95

    7.1: Assessing Your Organization's Readiness 97

    7.2. Developing a Remote Work Policy 102

    7.3. Revisiting Roles and Responsibilities 109

    7.4. Pilot Testing and Iteration 113

    7.5. Monitoring and Continuous Improvement 116

Epilogue: 121

References and Sources 123

Chapter 1: Understanding Hybrid and Fully Remote Teams

In recent years, the way we work has undergone a significant transformation, driven by advances in technology, changes in societal expectations, and, more recently, the global pandemic. As a result, hybrid and fully remote work models have become increasingly popular, challenging organizations to adapt their structures and strategies to this new reality.

The first chapter of this book aims to provide a foundational understanding of hybrid and fully remote work models, including their benefits, challenges, and key factors influencing organizational design. By exploring these topics, readers will gain valuable insights into the complexities of designing and managing organizations with remote and hybrid teams.

In Section 1.1, we will define the hybrid and remote work models, differentiating between the two and highlighting other variations, such as distributed teams and coworking spaces. Section 1.2 delves into the advantages and potential challenges of remote work, offering suggestions on how organizations can overcome obstacles and capitalize on the benefits. Finally, Section 1.3 examines the key factors influencing organizational design, including company culture, leadership style, industry and business model, and the size and growth of the organization.

As you read this chapter, consider how these concepts and ideas apply to your own organization or team. Reflect on the opportunities and challenges you face in embracing remote work and how a thoughtful approach to organizational design can help you navigate these complexities.

1.1. Defining Hybrid and Remote Work Models

The landscape of work has changed dramatically over the past decade, with technology enabling new ways of working and collaborating. As organizations adapt to these changes, it is essential to understand the various work models that have emerged. In this section, we'll explore the differences between hybrid and fully remote work models, as well as other variations that organizations may consider adopting.

Hybrid Work Model:

A hybrid work model is an arrangement where employees split their time between working remotely and working in a physical office space. This model provides a level of flexibility that allows employees to choose when and where they work, while still maintaining the benefits of in-person collaboration when needed.

In a hybrid model, employees may work remotely for a certain number of days per week or month, while spending the remaining days working from the office. Some organizations may even allow employees to determine their remote work schedule on a case-by-case basis, depending on individual needs and preferences. For example, an employee may choose to work remotely on Mondays and Fridays, while coming into the office on Tuesdays, Wednesdays, and Thursdays.

Hybrid work models can be particularly advantageous for organizations that want to maintain a physical office presence but also recognize the benefits of remote work. By allowing employees to work remotely part of the time, companies can save on office space and related expenses, while still benefiting from the camaraderie, teamwork, and face-to-face interactions that an office environment provides.

Fully Remote Work Model:

A fully remote work model, also known as a virtual or distributed work model, is an arrangement in which an organization operates without a centralized office. Instead, employees work from various locations, such as their homes, coworking spaces, or even from different countries. In this model, communication and collaboration primarily occur through virtual channels, such as video calls, instant messaging, and project management tools.

The fully remote work model offers several advantages for both employers and employees. For employers, this model can lead to significant cost savings, as there is no need to maintain a physical office space or cover expenses such as utilities and office supplies. Additionally, having a fully remote team allows organizations to tap into a wider pool of talent, as they can hire from virtually anywhere in the world.

For employees, the fully remote work model can provide a better work-life balance, as they can eliminate the time and stress associated with commuting. It also offers the flexibility to work in an environment that suits their individual needs and preferences, whether that's a quiet home office or a bustling coworking space.

Other Variations:

In addition to hybrid and fully remote work models, there are other variations that organizations may consider, depending on their specific needs and objectives. Some of these variations include:

Distributed teams: A distributed team is a group of employees who work from various locations, often across different time zones. This model can be a subset of a larger organization that has a physical office presence, or it can be the primary structure for a fully remote organization. Distributed teams rely heavily on communication and collaboration tools to stay connected and work effectively.

Satellite offices: Some organizations may choose to maintain multiple smaller offices or "satellites" in separate locations, rather than having one central office. This can be an effective way to support remote or hybrid work models, as employees can work from the satellite office that is closest to their home or preferred work location. Satellite offices can also help organizations expand their presence in different markets and attract talent from a wider geographic area.

Coworking spaces: Coworking spaces are shared office spaces that provide individuals and businesses with a flexible and cost-effective alternative to traditional office leases. These spaces typically offer a variety of amenities, such as high-speed internet, meeting rooms, and office equipment. Organizations with remote or hybrid teams may choose to provide their employees with memberships to coworking spaces, allowing them to work in a professional environment without the need for a dedicated office space.

Each of these variations offers unique benefits and challenges that organizations must consider when determining the best work model for their needs. Factors such as company culture, industry, size, and growth objectives will all play a role in shaping the organization's decision.

In conclusion, hybrid and fully remote work models have gained significant traction in recent years, driven by advances in technology and a growing recognition of the benefits that remote work can provide for both employers and employees. As organizations adapt to this new world of work, it's crucial to understand the different work models available and determine which approach best aligns with the organization's culture, goals, and objectives.

By offering a flexible and adaptable work environment, organizations can attract top talent, improve employee satisfaction and retention, and maintain a competitive edge in today's rapidly evolving business landscape. However, it's also important to recognize the potential challenges that come with remote work, such as communication barriers, collaboration difficulties, and maintaining a cohesive company culture.

In the next sections of this chapter, we will explore the benefits and challenges of remote work in greater detail, as well as discuss the key factors influencing organizational design in the context of hybrid and fully remote teams. By understanding these complexities, organizations can make informed decisions about their work models and implement effective strategies to support their remote and hybrid employees.

1.2. Benefits and Challenges

As we delve deeper into understanding hybrid and fully remote work models, it's essential to consider the benefits and challenges associated with each. By doing so, organizations can make informed decisions about which model best suits their needs and develop strategies to address potential obstacles.

Advantages of Remote Work:

Remote work offers several benefits for both employers and employees, including:

Cost savings for employers and employees: Remote work can significantly reduce overhead costs for organizations, as there is no need to maintain a large physical office space or cover expenses such as utilities and office supplies. Employees also save money by eliminating commuting costs and other work-related expenses.

Access to a wider talent pool: By allowing employees to work remotely, organizations can hire from virtually anywhere in the world, tapping into a diverse and skilled talent pool that may not have been accessible otherwise.

Increased employee satisfaction and retention: Remote work can lead to higher levels of job satisfaction, as employees have more control over their work environment and schedule. This, in turn, can lead to improved employee retention, as satisfied employees are more likely to stay with their current organization.

Improved work-life balance: Remote work allows employees to better balance their personal and professional lives, as they can eliminate the time and stress associated with commuting and have more flexibility in their daily schedules.

Environmental benefits: Remote work can reduce the environmental impact associated with commuting and office operations, leading to a smaller carbon footprint for organizations and employees alike.

Potential Challenges:

Despite the numerous benefits, remote work also presents several challenges that organizations must address, such as:

Communication barriers: Remote work can make communication more difficult, as employees are not physically present to engage in face-to-face conversations. This can lead to misunderstandings and reduced collaboration if not addressed proactively.

Collaboration difficulties: Working remotely can make it more challenging for employees to collaborate on projects, as they may need to navigate different time zones, communication preferences, and technological tools.

Building a cohesive company culture: Remote work can make it more difficult for organizations to maintain a strong company culture, as employees may feel isolated or disconnected from their colleagues and the organization's values.

Performance management and accountability: Remote work can make it more challenging for managers to monitor employee performance and ensure accountability, as they do not have the same level of visibility into employees' day-to-day activities.

Isolation and mental health concerns: Remote work can lead to feelings of isolation and loneliness for some employees, which can negatively impact their mental health and overall well-being.

Overcoming Obstacles:

To overcome the challenges associated with remote work, organizations can implement effective communication strategies, encourage team building and bonding, and provide necessary resources and support. Some strategies to consider include:

Implementing a robust communication framework that includes regular check-ins, team meetings, and one-on-one discussions between managers and employees.

Encouraging the use of collaboration tools, such as project management software, video conferencing platforms, and instant messaging apps, to facilitate communication and teamwork among remote employees.

Providing training and support for employees to develop their remote work skills, such as time management, self-discipline, and communication.

Organizing virtual team-building activities and social events to help employees connect with their colleagues and build a sense of camaraderie.

Offering mental health resources and support to address feelings of isolation and loneliness that may arise for remote employees.

By understanding the benefits and challenges associated with remote work, organizations can make informed decisions about their work models and implement strategies to support their remote and hybrid employees effectively. In the next section, we will explore the key factors influencing organizational design in the context of hybrid and fully remote teams.

1.3. Key Factors Influencing Organizational Design

As organizations consider adopting hybrid or fully remote work models, it's essential to understand the key factors that will influence their organizational design. These factors will play a significant role in determining how an organization structures its teams, manages its workforce, and creates a supportive and productive work environment.

Company Culture:

Company culture is the foundation upon which an organization is built, encompassing its core values, beliefs, and attitudes towards work. The organization's culture will significantly impact its approach to remote work and the degree of trust and autonomy it extends to employees. A culture that values collaboration, innovation, and flexibility will be better suited to adopting remote work models, whereas a culture that emphasizes control and strict adherence to rules may struggle to adapt.

Leadership Style:

The leadership style of an organization's management team will also play a crucial role in shaping its approach to remote work. Leaders who embrace a top-down decision-making process and exert a high degree of control and oversight may find it challenging to manage remote teams effectively. On the other hand, leaders who adopt a more democratic, bottom-up approach to decision-making and empower employees to take ownership of their work are more likely to succeed in creating an environment that supports remote work.

Industry and Business Model:

The industry in which an organization operates, and its underlying business model will also influence its ability to adopt remote work models. Some industries, such as technology and professional services, are better suited to remote work due to the nature of their work and the prevalence of digital tools and processes. In contrast, industries that rely heavily on physical presence or face-to-face interactions may find it more difficult to transition to remote work.

The role of technology and automation in an organization's operations can also impact its approach to remote work. Companies that leverage innovative technologies and automate routine tasks may find it easier to support remote employees, as these tools can facilitate communication, collaboration, and productivity regardless of location.

Competitive landscape and market dynamics will also play a role in an organization's approach to remote work. Companies operating in highly competitive markets or facing disruptive forces may be more likely to embrace remote work models as a means of gaining a competitive advantage and staying agile in the face of change.

Size and Growth of the Organization:

The size and growth trajectory of an organization will also influence its approach to remote work. Small businesses and startups may face unique challenges in implementing remote work models, such as limited resources and a lack of established processes and infrastructure. However, these organizations may also be more agile and adaptable, making it easier for them to embrace remote work and innovate quickly.

Larger organizations, on the other hand, may have more resources and infrastructure to support remote work but may struggle with the complexities of managing a distributed workforce and maintaining a cohesive company culture. Balancing growth and maintaining culture is a critical challenge for organizations of all sizes, and it's essential to consider how remote work models can support or hinder these objectives.

In conclusion, as organizations navigate the complexities of designing and managing teams in the context of hybrid and fully remote work models, it's essential to consider the key factors that influence their organizational design. By understanding how company culture, leadership style, industry and business model, and the size and growth of the organization impact their approach to remote work, companies can make informed decisions about their work models and develop strategies to create a supportive and productive environment for all employees.

Chapter 2: Designing an Effective Organizational Structure

The rise of remote and hybrid work models has revolutionized the way organizations operate, demanding a re-evaluation of traditional organizational structures to accommodate the unique challenges and opportunities presented by these new work environments. As companies adapt to the shifting landscape of work, it is essential to create an organizational structure that not only supports remote and hybrid employees but also fosters a culture of collaboration, adaptability, and trust. Designing an effective organizational structure is key to maintaining employee engagement, productivity, and satisfaction while ensuring that the organization remains competitive and agile in a rapidly changing world.

In this chapter, we will delve into the critical aspects of designing an effective organizational structure for remote and hybrid workforces. We will explore the differences between traditional and agile organizational structures, providing an in-depth analysis of their pros and cons in the context of remote and hybrid work environments. Through this exploration, we will shed light on the principles of organizational design that can help organizations create structures that are better suited to the unique needs and challenges presented by remote and hybrid work models.

Furthermore, we will discuss practical strategies for implementing a remote-friendly organizational structure that not only addresses the unique needs of remote and hybrid workforces but also promotes a culture of collaboration, communication, and adaptability. These strategies will encompass areas such as decentralized decision-making, cross-functional collaboration, employee well-being, and leveraging technology and tools to support remote work.

By the end of this chapter, readers will gain valuable insights into the key components of designing an effective organizational structure for remote and hybrid workforces, as well as practical tools and strategies for implementing a remote-friendly structure within their own organizations. This knowledge will be instrumental in helping organizations adapt to the evolving world of work and ensure that they remain competitive, innovative, and agile in the face of change.

2.1. Traditional vs. Agile Organizational Structures: In-depth Comparison and Considerations for Remote Work

To create an effective remote-friendly organizational structure, it is crucial to understand the differences between traditional and agile organizational structures, as well as the benefits and drawbacks of each approach in the context of remote and hybrid work environments.

Traditional Organizational Structures

Traditional organizational structures are characterized by a hierarchical approach, featuring well-defined roles and responsibilities, clear chains of command, and a centralized decision-making process. In these structures, employees are often grouped into departments based on their functions, such as marketing, finance, or operations.

Pros of Traditional Structures:

1. Stability: Traditional structures provide stability and predictability within an organization, as roles and responsibilities are clearly defined, and decision-making processes are well-established.

2. Clear career progression: With well-defined roles and a clear hierarchy, employees have a better understanding of their potential career path within the organization.

3. Control and oversight: Centralized decision-making allows for greater control and oversight, ensuring that decisions align with the organization's strategic objectives.

Cons of Traditional Structures:

1. Rigidity: Traditional structures can be rigid and inflexible, making it difficult for organizations to adapt quickly to changes in the business environment.

2. Silos: Departmentalization within traditional structures can lead to silos, where teams become isolated and fail to communicate or collaborate effectively with other departments.

3. Bureaucracy: The hierarchical nature of traditional structures often results in bureaucracy, slowing down decision-making processes and hindering innovation.

Agile Organizational Structures

Agile organizational structures prioritize flexibility, adaptability, and collaboration. Rather than rigid hierarchies, agile structures often feature cross-functional teams, decentralized decision-making, and a focus on continuous improvement. In these organizations, employees are empowered to make decisions, experiment, and adapt to changes in the business environment.

Pros of Agile Structures:

1. Adaptability: Agile structures enable organizations to respond quickly to changes in the business environment and remain competitive.

2. Collaboration and innovation: Cross-functional teams and decentralized decision-making processes promote collaboration and innovation, as employees are encouraged to share ideas, learn from one another, and experiment with innovative approaches.

3. Employee empowerment: Employees in agile organizations have greater autonomy and decision-making authority, leading to increased engagement, motivation, and job satisfaction.

Cons of Agile Structures:

1. Uncertainty: Decentralized decision-making and greater employee autonomy can create uncertainty and ambiguity

within the organization, as roles and responsibilities may be less clearly defined.

2. Coordination challenges: Agile structures may require more coordination and communication among teams, which can be challenging, particularly in remote and hybrid work environments.

3. Potential loss of control: With greater autonomy and decision-making authority, there is a risk of losing control over the organization's strategic direction and decision-making processes.

Considerations for Remote and Hybrid Work Environments

When designing an organizational structure for remote and hybrid work models, it is important to consider the unique challenges and opportunities these environments present. Agile structures may be better suited for remote work, as they promote collaboration, communication, and adaptability, which are essential for success in remote and hybrid environments.

Communication and collaboration: In remote and hybrid work environments, effective communication and collaboration are critical to maintaining productivity and employee engagement. Agile structures, with their emphasis on cross-functional teams and decentralized decision-making, encourage employees to work together, share ideas, and support one another. This fosters a culture of collaboration that can help overcome the challenges of remote work, such as feelings of isolation and disconnection.

Adaptability: Remote and hybrid work models require organizations to be adaptable and flexible in response to changes in the business environment, employee needs, and technological advancements. Agile structures, with their focus on continuous improvement and adaptability, enable organizations to pivot quickly and respond effectively to these changes. This adaptability is essential for success in remote and hybrid work environments, where organizations must be prepared to adjust their strategies, processes, and tools to accommodate the evolving needs of their workforce and the changing business landscape.

Autonomy and trust: Remote and hybrid work environments demand a greater degree of trust and autonomy for employees. Agile structures empower employees to make decisions, take ownership of their work, and contribute to the organization's strategic direction. This fosters a culture of trust and autonomy, which is crucial for maintaining employee motivation, engagement, and satisfaction in remote and hybrid work settings.

Technology and tools: Both traditional and agile organizational structures can benefit from leveraging technology and tools to support remote and hybrid work. However, agile structures, with their emphasis on collaboration and adaptability, may be better equipped to take full advantage of digital tools and platforms that facilitate communication, project management, and knowledge sharing.

Employee well-being and work-life balance: Remote and hybrid work models can present challenges to employee well-being and work-life balance. Agile structures, with their focus on flexibility and adaptability, may be better suited to supporting employees in maintaining a healthy balance between their work and personal lives. By fostering a culture that values work-life balance and providing resources and support to help employees navigate the challenges of remote work, organizations with agile structures can promote employee well-being and reduce the risk of burnout.

Talent acquisition and retention: In an increasingly competitive talent market, organizations must prioritize attracting and retaining top talent. Agile structures, with their emphasis on flexibility, adaptability, and employee empowerment, may be more attractive to potential candidates and help organizations retain their top performers. Additionally, remote and hybrid work models can broaden the talent pool, enabling organizations to hire from a more diverse and geographically dispersed group of candidates.

In conclusion, when designing an organizational structure for remote and hybrid work environments, it is essential to weigh the benefits and drawbacks of both traditional and agile approaches. Organizations that prioritize adaptability, collaboration, and employee empowerment may find that an agile structure is better suited to their needs in a remote or hybrid work context. By embracing agile principles and leveraging technology and tools to support remote work, organizations can create an effective organizational structure that enables employees to thrive and remain productive in a rapidly changing business landscape.

2.2: Principles of Organizational Design for Hybrid and Fully Remote Teams

Designing an effective organizational structure for hybrid and fully remote teams requires a thorough understanding of the core principles of organizational design. These principles serve as guiding factors in creating a structure that is not only functional but also supports collaboration, communication, adaptability, and employee well-being. In this section, we will discuss six key principles of organizational design that are crucial for creating an effective structure for hybrid and fully remote workforces.

1. Align with organizational strategy and goals: The organizational structure should be designed to support the overall strategy and goals of the organization. It is essential to consider how the structure will facilitate the achievement of strategic objectives and help the organization remain competitive in its industry. When designing an organizational structure for remote and hybrid teams, consider how the structure will enable employees to work effectively towards shared goals and maintain a strong connection to the organization's mission and vision.

2. Foster collaboration and communication: An effective organizational structure should promote collaboration and communication across teams and departments, ensuring that employees have the necessary channels and tools to share information, ideas, and feedback. In remote and hybrid work environments, communication can be more challenging due to the physical distance between team members. Therefore, it is

crucial to create a structure that encourages open communication, leverages technology to facilitate collaboration, and provides opportunities for both synchronous and asynchronous communication.

3. Encourage autonomy and decentralize decision-making: Remote and hybrid work models often require a greater degree of autonomy for employees. An effective organizational structure should empower employees to make decisions, take ownership of their work, and contribute to the organization's strategic direction. Decentralizing decision-making processes can help create a more agile and adaptable organization, as employees are better able to respond quickly to changes in the business environment and collaborate effectively with their colleagues. This principle is particularly relevant for organizations adopting an agile organizational structure, which prioritizes flexibility, adaptability, and employee empowerment.

4. Prioritize adaptability and flexibility: An effective organizational structure should be adaptable and flexible, allowing the organization to respond quickly to changes in the business environment, employee needs, and technological advancements. This is especially important in remote and hybrid work models, where organizations must be prepared to adjust their strategies, processes, and tools to accommodate the evolving needs of their workforce and the changing business landscape. Designing an organizational structure with adaptability and flexibility in mind can help organizations remain agile and competitive in a rapidly changing world.

5. Support employee well-being and work-life balance: An effective organizational structure should prioritize employee well-being and work-life balance, ensuring that employees have the necessary resources and support to maintain a healthy balance between their work and personal lives. In remote and hybrid work environments, employee well-being can be more challenging to address due to factors such as isolation, lack of social interaction, and blurred boundaries between work and home. It is essential to design an organizational structure that considers these challenges and provides the necessary support and resources to help employees maintain a healthy work-life balance.

6. Streamline processes and minimize bureaucracy: An effective organizational structure should minimize bureaucracy and streamline processes, ensuring that decision-making is efficient and that employees can focus on their core tasks and responsibilities. In remote and hybrid work environments, it is particularly important to minimize bureaucracy, as it can hinder communication, collaboration, and adaptability. Designing an organizational structure that prioritizes streamlined processes and reduces bureaucratic obstacles can help organizations remain agile and responsive in a remote or hybrid work context.

In conclusion, understanding and applying these principles of organizational design is crucial for creating an effective structure for hybrid and fully remote teams. By aligning the organizational structure with the company's strategy and goals, fostering collaboration and communication, encouraging autonomy and decentralized decision-making, prioritizing adaptability and flexibility, supporting employee well-being and work-life balance, and streamlining processes to minimize bureaucracy, organizations can create an environment that supports the unique needs and challenges of remote and hybrid workforces.

It is important to note that these principles are not one-size-fits-all solutions but rather serve as guidelines for organizations to consider when designing their own unique structures. Each organization must evaluate its specific needs, industry, workforce, and culture to determine the best approach to organizational design.

When implementing these principles, organizations should also be prepared to iterate and adapt their structures as needed. Remote and hybrid work environments are constantly evolving, and organizations must be willing to learn from their experiences, gather feedback from employees, and adjust as necessary to ensure the ongoing success of their remote-friendly structures.

Furthermore, organizations should consider conducting regular assessments of their structures to ensure that they continue to align with the organization's strategy and goals, support collaboration and communication, empower employees, and prioritize adaptability and employee well-being. This ongoing evaluation and adjustment process will help organizations remain agile and responsive in an ever-changing business landscape, ultimately leading to increased success and competitive advantage.

In summary, applying the principles of organizational design to remote and hybrid teams is a critical aspect of creating an environment that supports collaboration, communication, adaptability, and employee well-being. By understanding and applying these principles, organizations can create effective structures that enable their remote and hybrid workforces to thrive, driving increased productivity, employee satisfaction, and overall business success.

2.3: Implementing a Remote-Friendly Organizational Structure

Once you have a solid understanding of the principles of organizational design, it's time to put these ideas into practice and implement a remote-friendly organizational structure. In this chapter, we will outline a step-by-step approach to implementing a remote-friendly organizational structure that supports your hybrid and fully remote workforce, while also promoting communication, collaboration, and employee well-being.

1. Assess your current organizational structure: Before you can implement a remote-friendly organizational structure, you need to assess your current structure to identify its strengths, weaknesses, and opportunities for improvement. This assessment should include a review of existing roles, responsibilities, communication channels, and processes to determine how well they align with the principles of organizational design and the specific needs of your remote and hybrid workforce.

2. Define your desired organizational structure: Based on your assessment, define the desired organizational structure that will best support your remote and hybrid workforce. Consider the following factors when defining your desired structure:

- Alignment with your organization's strategy and goals

- Facilitation of collaboration and communication

- Encouragement of autonomy and decentralized decision-making

- Adaptability and flexibility to accommodate changing business needs and workforce dynamics

- Support for employee well-being and work-life balance

- Streamlined processes and minimized bureaucracy

3. Develop a plan for transitioning to the new structure: With your desired organizational structure defined, develop a detailed plan for transitioning from your current structure to the new remote-friendly structure. This plan should outline the specific changes to roles, responsibilities, communication channels, and processes that will be necessary to implement the new structure. It should also include a timeline for implementing these changes and any necessary resources, such as training or technology, which will be required to support the transition.

4. Communicate the plan to employees: To ensure a smooth transition to the new remote-friendly organizational structure, it's essential to communicate the plan to all employees. This communication should include a clear explanation of the reasons for the change, the benefits of the new structure, and the specific steps that will be taken to implement the new structure. Be transparent and open to addressing any concerns or questions employees may have about the transition.

5. Implement the new structure: With a clear plan in place and employee buy-in secured, it's time to implement the new remote-friendly organizational structure. This process may involve changes to roles, responsibilities, reporting lines, and communication channels. It may also require the introduction of

new technologies or tools to facilitate collaboration and communication in the remote or hybrid work environment. Be prepared to provide support and training as necessary to help employees adapt to the new structure.

6. Monitor and evaluate the effectiveness of the new structure: As you implement the new remote-friendly organizational structure, it's essential to monitor and evaluate its effectiveness. This evaluation should include regular check-ins with employees to gather feedback on their experiences with the new structure and any challenges they may be facing. It should also include a review of key performance indicators (KPIs) related to communication, collaboration, productivity, and employee well-being to assess the impact of the new structure on these areas.

7. Iterate and adjust as needed: Based on your evaluation of the new remote-friendly organizational structure, be prepared to adjust and iterate as needed to address any challenges or opportunities for improvement. This may involve refining roles and responsibilities, adjusting communication channels, or implementing new tools or processes to better support remote and hybrid work. Remember that implementing a remote-friendly organizational structure is an ongoing process that requires flexibility, adaptability, and a commitment to continuous improvement.

In conclusion, implementing a remote-friendly organizational structure is a critical step in supporting the unique needs and challenges of hybrid and fully remote workforces. By following the step-by-step approach outlined in this chapter, organizations can create a remote-friendly organizational structure that promotes communication, collaboration, adaptability, and employee well-being, ultimately leading to increased productivity, employee satisfaction, and overall business success.

8. Foster a culture of continuous improvement: As your organization adapts to the remote-friendly organizational structure, it's important to foster a culture of continuous improvement. Encourage employees to share their ideas, challenges, and successes in the remote and hybrid work environment. Use this feedback to make ongoing adjustments to your structure, processes, and tools to ensure that your organization continues to evolve and improve over time.

9. Stay informed about industry trends and best practices: The landscape of remote and hybrid work is constantly evolving, and it's essential for organizations to stay informed about industry trends, best practices, and emerging technologies. By staying up to date on these developments, you can ensure that your remote-friendly organizational structure remains relevant, effective, and competitive in the ever-changing business landscape.

10. Be prepared to adapt to future changes: Implementing a remote-friendly organizational structure is not a one-time effort, but rather an ongoing process that requires organizations to remain agile and responsive to changes in the business environment, workforce dynamics, and employee needs. As your organization grows and evolves, be prepared to reassess and adapt your remote-friendly organizational structure to ensure that it continues to support your remote and hybrid workforce effectively.

By following these steps and maintaining a commitment to continuous improvement, your organization can successfully implement a remote-friendly organizational structure that supports the unique needs and challenges of your hybrid and fully remote workforce. This, in turn, will help your organization unlock the numerous benefits of remote and hybrid work, including increased productivity, employee satisfaction, and overall business success.

In the subsequent chapters of this book, we will delve deeper into the specific strategies, tools, and techniques that can help organizations optimize their remote-friendly organizational structures, such as building a robust communication framework, leveraging technology for effective collaboration, and fostering employee engagement and well-being in remote and hybrid work environments. By applying these strategies in conjunction with the principles and steps outlined in this chapter, your organization will be well-equipped to navigate the complexities of remote and hybrid work and thrive in the modern business landscape.

Chapter 3: Communication and Collaboration

In the previous chapters, we explored the foundations of hybrid and fully remote teams, the key factors influencing organizational design, and the principles behind implementing a remote-friendly organizational structure. As we move forward, we will address another essential aspect of managing hybrid and fully remote teams: communication and collaboration. The shift to remote work brings unique challenges to the way team members interact, share information, and work together to achieve common goals. In this chapter, we will focus on strategies for building a solid communication framework, leveraging technology for effective collaboration, and fostering a culture of openness and transparency.

3.1: Building a Communication Framework

An effective communication framework is the backbone of any successful hybrid or remote team. It ensures that team members stay connected, informed, and engaged, regardless of their location. In this section, we will discuss the key components of a robust communication framework and provide practical tips for implementing these components in your organization.

1. Establish clear communication channels: The first step in building a communication framework is to define the channels through which team members will communicate. These channels should be clear, accessible, and tailored to the specific

needs of your team. Common communication channels include email, instant messaging platforms, video conferencing tools, and project management software. When choosing communication channels, consider the following:

   a. Purpose: Determine the primary purpose of each channel (e.g., real-time collaboration, formal communication, or project updates) and ensure that team members use the channels accordingly.

   b. Accessibility: Ensure that all team members have access to the chosen communication channels and are comfortable using them.

   c. Security: Choose communication channels that meet your organization's security requirements, particularly when dealing with sensitive or confidential information.

2. Set communication norms and expectations: To facilitate effective communication, establish clear norms and expectations for how team members should use the various communication channels. This might include:

   a. Response times: Set expectations for how quickly team members should respond to messages or requests, depending on the urgency and nature of the communication.

   b. Availability: Encourage team members to share their availability (e.g., working hours, time zones, or preferred communication times) and respect each other's boundaries.

   c. Etiquette: Establish guidelines for professional and respectful communication, including the use of appropriate language, tone, and style.

3. Implement regular check-ins and meetings: Regular check-ins and meetings are essential for keeping team members connected, informed, and engaged. These check-ins can take various forms, such as daily stand-ups, weekly team meetings, or monthly all-hands meetings. When scheduling check-ins and meetings, consider the following:

   a. Frequency: Determine the appropriate frequency for check-ins and meetings based on your team's needs, workload, and communication preferences.

   b. Format: Choose a format that best supports your team's goals and objectives, such as video conferencing, audio calls, or written updates.

   c. Agenda: Develop a clear agenda for each check-in or meeting to ensure that time is used effectively and that all relevant topics are covered.

4. Encourage open and inclusive communication: An essential aspect of a robust communication framework is fostering an environment where team members feel comfortable sharing their thoughts, ideas, and concerns. This can be achieved by:

   a. Promoting psychological safety: Create a safe space for team members to express their opinions without fear of judgment or retaliation.

   b. Encouraging active listening: Encourage team members to practice active listening and seek to understand each other's perspectives before responding or offering solutions.

   c. Valuing diverse perspectives: Recognize and appreciate the unique contributions and perspectives that each team member brings to the table, regardless of their background, experience, or expertise.

By following these guidelines and implementing a well-structured communication framework, your organization will be better equipped to handle the challenges associated with hybrid and fully remote teams. It's essential to remember that effective communication is an ongoing process, and organizations should regularly review and update their communication strategies to accommodate the evolving needs of their teams.

Foster a culture of feedback: In a remote or hybrid work environment, feedback plays a crucial role in maintaining open lines of communication and ensuring continuous improvement. Encourage team members to share feedback with one another regularly, both in structured settings (e.g., performance reviews) and informally during day-to-day interactions. Consider the following:

a. Feedback tools: Leverage tools and platforms that facilitate feedback sharing, such as anonymous feedback surveys or dedicated feedback channels on team communication platforms.

b. Training and support: Provide training and resources to help team members develop effective feedback skills, including how to give and receive constructive criticism.

c. Celebrate successes: Encourage team members to share and celebrate their accomplishments, as well as the achievements of their colleagues, to foster a culture of recognition and appreciation.

Establish communication routines: To further strengthen your communication framework, establish routines that promote regular interaction and information sharing among team members. These routines can include:

a. Daily or weekly updates: Encourage team members to share regular updates on their progress, challenges, and priorities.

b. Virtual team-building activities: Schedule regular virtual team-building activities, such as online games, coffee breaks, or social events, to help team members connect and build relationships outside of work-related tasks.

c. Cross-functional collaboration: Foster collaboration between different departments or teams by organizing cross-functional projects, meetings, or workshops.

In conclusion, building an effective communication framework is essential for the success of hybrid and fully remote teams. By establishing clear communication channels, setting norms and expectations, implementing regular check-ins and meetings, and fostering open and inclusive communication, your organization will be well-positioned to overcome the communication challenges associated with remote work. Remember that communication is an ongoing process, and it's crucial to regularly review and adapt your strategies to ensure they continue to meet the needs of your team.

3.2: Leveraging Technology for Effective Collaboration

The rapid advancement of technology has played a significant role in the rise of remote and hybrid work models. As organizations navigate the complexities of managing geographically dispersed teams, leveraging the right technology becomes crucial to ensure seamless communication and collaboration. This chapter explores various tools and platforms that can help organizations maximize efficiency and productivity in hybrid and fully remote work environments.

1. Communication Tools:

Effective communication is the backbone of successful remote and hybrid teams. Various communication tools can help bridge the gap between team members and facilitate real-time interaction. Some popular communication tools include:

   a. Instant messaging: Slack, Microsoft Teams, and Google Chat are examples of instant messaging platforms that enable real-time communication, file sharing, and collaboration. These tools can help reduce email clutter and provide a more informal, conversational way of communication.

   b. Video conferencing: Video conferencing tools such as Zoom, Google Meet, and Microsoft Teams allow teams to connect visually, share screens, and hold virtual meetings or presentations. Video conferencing is essential for maintaining a sense of connection and camaraderie among remote team members.

c. VoIP and phone systems: Voice over Internet Protocol (VoIP) services like Skype or Google Voice can provide cost-effective phone services for remote teams, allowing team members to make and receive calls through their internet connection.

2. Project Management and Collaboration Tools

Managing projects and tasks efficiently is crucial for remote teams to stay on track and meet deadlines. Project management and collaboration tools can help streamline workflows, track progress, and improve overall productivity. Some popular options include:

a. Task and project management: Tools like Trello, Asana, and Monday.com offer intuitive, visual platforms for organizing tasks, assigning responsibilities, and tracking progress. These tools can help teams prioritize tasks, manage workloads, and ensure deadlines are met.

b. Document collaboration: Platforms such as Google Workspace, Microsoft Office 365, and Notion provide cloud-based solutions for document creation, collaboration, and sharing. Team members can work on documents simultaneously, leave comments, and track changes in real-time, fostering a more collaborative work environment.

c. File sharing and storage: Cloud storage solutions like Dropbox, Google Drive, and OneDrive enable teams to store, share, and access files and documents from any device, ensuring everyone has the necessary resources to complete their tasks.

3. Time and Resource Management Tools

Effectively managing time and resources is essential for remote teams to maintain productivity and stay on schedule. Time and resource management tools can help teams monitor workloads, allocate resources, and optimize workflows. Some popular options include:

   a. Time tracking: Time tracking tools such as Toggl, Harvest, and Clockify enable team members to track the time they spend on tasks and projects, providing valuable insights into work patterns, productivity levels, and areas for improvement.

   b. Resource allocation: Platforms like Float, Mavenlink, and Resource Guru help organizations optimize resource allocation by providing a clear overview of team members' workloads, project timelines, and resource availability. These tools can help managers make informed decisions about task assignments and workload distribution.

   c. Calendar management: Calendar management tools like Google Calendar, Microsoft Outlook, and Calendly help teams coordinate schedules, set up meetings, and manage deadlines. By centralizing calendars and streamlining scheduling processes, teams can stay organized and avoid double bookings.

4. Virtual Whiteboards and Brainstorming Tools

Remote and hybrid teams often miss the spontaneous brainstorming sessions and whiteboard discussions that take place in physical workspaces. Virtual whiteboard and brainstorming tools can help recreate these collaborative experiences by providing an online space for team members to share ideas, sketch concepts, and collaborate on problem-solving. Some popular options include:

a. Virtual whiteboards: Tools like Miro, MURAL, and Microsoft Whiteboard offer digital canvases for teams to collaborate visually, create diagrams, and brainstorm ideas in real-time. These platforms often include a range of templates and pre-built elements to facilitate the creative process.

b. Mind mapping: Mind mapping tools like XMind, MindMeister, and Coggle help teams visually organize and structure complex ideas, enabling a more effective brainstorming process. These tools allow for easy collaboration and can be integrated with other project management platforms for seamless workflow management.

5. Security and Compliance Tools

As organizations increasingly rely on digital tools and platforms for remote work, ensuring the security and privacy of company data becomes a top priority. Security and compliance tools can help protect sensitive information and maintain regulatory compliance. Some popular options include:

a. VPNs: Virtual Private Networks (VPNs) like ExpressVPN, NordVPN, and Surfshark provide a secure, encrypted connection for remote workers to access company resources and protect data from potential threats.

b. Password managers: Password managers like LastPass, Dashlane, and 1Password help teams securely store and share login credentials, reducing the risk of unauthorized access to company accounts.

c. Compliance management: Platforms like ZenGRC, LogicGate, and Onspring offer comprehensive solutions for managing regulatory compliance and risk assessment, helping organizations maintain compliance in a remote work environment.

In conclusion, leveraging technology is crucial for fostering effective communication and collaboration among hybrid and remote teams. Organizations must carefully evaluate their needs and select the right tools and platforms that align with their work processes and culture. By investing in the right technology stack, companies can ensure a seamless transition to remote work, improve productivity, and maintain a high level of employee satisfaction.

3.3: Encouraging a Culture of Openness and Transparency

Creating a culture of openness and transparency is critical for the success of hybrid and fully remote teams. In this new work environment, organizations must foster trust and encourage open communication to ensure that employees feel connected, informed, and engaged. This chapter will discuss the importance of openness and transparency in remote work settings, strategies for promoting these values, and best practices for maintaining a transparent organizational culture.

1. The Importance of Openness and Transparency in Remote Work

Openness and transparency are essential for building trust and maintaining effective communication among remote teams. When employees feel that information is being shared openly and decisions are being made transparently, they are more likely to trust their colleagues and leaders. This trust is crucial for remote work, as employees often have less face-to-face interaction and rely more heavily on virtual communication channels.

A transparent culture also promotes accountability and collaboration among team members. When employees understand the rationale behind decisions and have access to relevant information, they can contribute more effectively to the decision-making process and feel more invested in the organization's success. Transparency in communication helps prevent misunderstandings and fosters a sense of unity, even when team members are physically dispersed.

2. Strategies for Promoting Openness and Transparency

Implementing a culture of openness and transparency in remote work environments requires deliberate effort and strategic planning. Here are some strategies for promoting these values in hybrid and fully remote teams:

   a. Set clear expectations: Ensure that employees understand the importance of openness and transparency and are aware of the organization's commitment to these values. Communicate expectations around information sharing, collaboration, and decision-making, and provide guidance on how to uphold these principles in daily work.

   b. Encourage open communication: Foster a culture where employees feel comfortable sharing their thoughts, ideas, and concerns. Encourage team members to ask questions, provide feedback, and participate in discussions. Create opportunities for open dialogue through regular team meetings, town halls, and informal chat channels.

   c. Share information proactively: Make it a priority to share relevant information with employees in a timely manner. This includes updates on company performance, strategic initiatives, and organizational changes. Use a variety of communication channels, such as email, intranet, and virtual meetings, to ensure that information reaches all team members.

   d. Involve employees in decision-making: Encourage employee participation in decision-making processes by soliciting their input and feedback. This not only promotes transparency but also helps to build trust and foster a sense of ownership among team members.

   e. Recognize and reward openness: Acknowledge and celebrate instances of openness and transparency within the organization. Recognize employees who demonstrate these values and provide positive reinforcement to encourage their continued practice.

3. Best Practices for Maintaining a Transparent Organizational Culture

Maintaining a culture of openness and transparency requires ongoing effort and commitment from all levels of the organization. Here are some best practices to help sustain this culture in hybrid and fully remote teams:

a. Lead by example: Leaders play a critical role in fostering a culture of openness and transparency. They should model these values by communicating openly, sharing information, and involving employees in decision-making processes.

b. Regularly reassess communication channels: Evaluate the effectiveness of your communication channels and tools to ensure that they are supporting a transparent work environment. Adjust as needed and consider adopting new technologies that facilitate open communication and information sharing.

c. Monitor and address potential barriers: Be vigilant about identifying and addressing any barriers to openness and transparency within the organization. This might include addressing interpersonal conflicts, resolving technology issues, or providing additional training and resources to support effective communication.

d. Gather feedback and make improvements: Regularly solicit feedback from employees on the organization's culture of openness and transparency. Use this information to identify areas for improvement and implement changes as needed. Encourage a continuous improvement mindset to ensure that the organization is always working towards maintaining and enhancing its transparent culture.

e. Promote psychological safety: Create an environment where employees feel comfortable expressing their thoughts and ideas without fear of judgment or negative consequences. A psychologically safe work environment is a key factor in fostering a culture of openness and transparency.

f. Provide training and support: Offer training and resources to help employees understand the importance of openness and transparency and develop the necessary skills to uphold these values. This may include workshops, webinars, or online resources focused on effective communication, collaboration, and decision-making in remote work settings.

g. Celebrate successes and learn from failures: Encourage a culture of learning by recognizing successes in promoting openness and transparency, as well as discussing and learning from failures. This approach helps to reinforce the value of transparency and demonstrates the organization's commitment to continuous improvement.

In conclusion, encouraging a culture of openness and transparency is crucial for the success of hybrid and fully remote teams. By implementing strategic initiatives, promoting best practices, and continuously assessing and improving the organization's transparent culture, companies can foster trust, collaboration, and employee engagement in remote work environments. This, in turn, leads to improved productivity, innovation, and overall organizational performance.

Chapter 4: Performance Management in Hybrid and Remote Teams

In today's rapidly evolving business landscape, organizations are increasingly recognizing the value of hybrid and fully remote work models. As these models gain traction, it is essential for companies to effectively manage the performance of their employees to ensure continued productivity, innovation, and overall success. Chapter 4 delves into the critical aspects of performance management in hybrid and remote teams, providing a comprehensive guide to setting clear expectations, monitoring and measuring performance, and conducting feedback and performance reviews.

Performance management is a continuous process that involves setting expectations, providing ongoing feedback, and measuring employee performance to ensure alignment with organizational goals and objectives. It plays a crucial role in maintaining employee engagement, fostering professional growth, and driving overall business success. In hybrid and remote work environments, where physical distance and varying work schedules can present unique challenges, effective performance management is more important than ever.

As we explore performance management in hybrid and remote teams, we will examine the key elements that contribute to a successful performance management system. These include setting clear expectations and goals, ensuring employees understand their roles and responsibilities, and maintaining open lines of communication for ongoing feedback and support.

In Section 4.1, we will discuss the importance of setting clear expectations and goals for remote employees. Establishing a clear understanding of what is expected of employees, both individually and as part of the team, is crucial in maintaining productivity and engagement in remote work environments. We will explore the process of setting goals and objectives, as well as techniques for effectively communicating expectations to employees.

Section 4.2 focuses on monitoring and measuring employee performance in hybrid and remote teams. We will explore various performance indicators and metrics that can be used to gauge employee performance, as well as tools and technologies that can help managers track and assess progress. We will also discuss the importance of maintaining a balance between monitoring performance and preserving employee autonomy and trust.

Finally, in Section 4.3, we will delve into the process of providing feedback and conducting performance reviews in hybrid and remote work environments. We will examine the benefits of regular feedback and performance discussions, as well as best practices for conducting effective performance reviews that support employee growth and development.

As organizations continue to adopt hybrid and remote work models, it is essential to adapt performance management practices to effectively support employees in these environments. By understanding and implementing the principles discussed in this chapter, companies can promote a culture of high performance, continuous improvement, and employee engagement across their hybrid and remote teams.

4.1: Setting Clear Expectations and Goals

Setting clear expectations and goals is a fundamental aspect of performance management in any work environment. However, it becomes even more critical in hybrid and remote teams, where employees may face unique challenges in terms of communication, collaboration, and staying connected to the broader organization. In this section, we will discuss the importance of establishing and communicating expectations and goals in hybrid and remote work settings, as well as strategies for doing so effectively.

1. The Importance of Clear Expectations and Goals

Clear expectations and goals serve as the foundation for successful performance management. They provide employees with a roadmap for success, outlining what is expected of them and the standards they must meet. They also offer a basis for ongoing feedback, performance evaluation, and professional growth. In hybrid and remote work environments, where employees may work in different locations and time zones, clear expectations and goals are essential to ensure:

a. Alignment: Ensuring that employees understand their roles and responsibilities and how they contribute to the organization's overall objectives.

b. Accountability: Providing a framework for holding employees accountable for their performance and empowering them to take ownership of their work.

c. Engagement: Enhancing employee engagement by creating a sense of purpose and direction, as well as opportunities for growth and development.

d. Collaboration: Facilitating effective collaboration and coordination among team members by clarifying roles, responsibilities, and expectations.

e. Performance Evaluation: Serving as the basis for evaluating employee performance, providing feedback, and identifying areas for improvement.

2. Setting Expectations and Goals: A Step-by-Step Process

Setting expectations and goals in hybrid and remote teams involves a structured process that includes the following steps:

a. Define Organizational Objectives: Start by defining the organization's overall objectives and strategy. This will serve as the foundation for setting expectations and goals for individual employees and teams.

b. Identify Key Performance Indicators (KPIs): Determine the KPIs that will be used to measure performance and success. These should be aligned with the organization's objectives and relevant to the specific roles and responsibilities of employees.

c. Set SMART Goals: Set Specific, Measurable, Achievable, Relevant, and Time-bound (SMART) goals for each employee or team. These goals should be directly tied to the organization's objectives and KPIs and clearly defined in terms of scope, timeframe, and expected outcomes.

d. Communicate Expectations and Goals: Clearly communicate expectations and goals to employees, ensuring they understand their roles, responsibilities, and performance targets. This can be done through one-on-one discussions, team meetings, written documentation, or a combination of these methods.

e. Align Expectations and Goals with Resources and Support: Ensure employees have the necessary resources, tools, and support to meet their expectations and goals. This may include providing access to technology, training, and ongoing support from managers and colleagues.

f. Review and Update Expectations and Goals Regularly: Periodically review and update expectations and goals to ensure they remain relevant and aligned with the organization's evolving objectives and strategy. This may involve setting new goals, adjusting existing ones, or revisiting KPIs as needed.

3. Strategies for Setting Expectations and Goals in Hybrid and Remote Teams

Implementing clear expectations and goals in hybrid and remote teams requires a thoughtful approach that accounts for the unique challenges and opportunities of these work environments. Some strategies for doing so effectively include:

a. Leverage Technology: Use technology to facilitate communication, collaboration, and goal setting. This may include project management tools, communication platforms, and goal-setting software that enable employees to stay connected and informed.

b. Emphasize Flexibility: Recognize that hybrid and remote employees may have different work schedules, time zones, and personal circumstances. Be flexible in setting expectations and goals and provide guidance and support where required.

c. opportunities for employees to adjust their work hours, deadlines, or workload as needed, while still meeting the overall objectives.

d. Focus on Outcomes: In hybrid and remote work environments, it's essential to focus on outcomes and results rather than simply the amount of time spent working. Set goals based on deliverables and results and allow employees the autonomy to manage their work schedules and processes to achieve those goals.

e. Foster a Culture of Trust: Establishing trust between employees and management is critical in remote and hybrid work environments. Trust enables employees to feel confident in their abilities to meet expectations and goals and allows management to provide employees with the autonomy they need to succeed.

f. Provide Regular Feedback: Ensure that employees receive regular feedback on their performance, both in terms of meeting expectations and achieving goals. This can be done through scheduled check-ins, performance reviews, or informal conversations. Feedback should be constructive, specific, and focused on areas for improvement or growth.

g. Encourage Employee Input: Involve employees in the process of setting expectations and goals. This can help create a sense of ownership and buy-in, as well as ensure that goals are realistic and achievable given the employee's unique circumstances and expertise.

h. Adapt to Individual Needs: Recognize that employees may have different learning styles, communication preferences, and work habits. Be prepared to adapt expectations and goals accordingly and provide tailored support to help employees succeed.

i. Promote Collaboration: Encourage collaboration and teamwork by setting shared goals and expectations for teams, departments, or the entire organization. This can help create a sense of shared responsibility and accountability, as well as foster a supportive work environment.

j. Monitor Progress: Regularly monitor employee progress towards their expectations and goals and adjust as needed. This may involve providing additional support, resources, or training, or adjusting expectations and goals to better align with the organization's objectives.

In conclusion, setting clear expectations and goals is crucial for effective performance management in hybrid and remote teams. By following the steps and strategies outlined in this section, organizations can ensure that employees have a clear understanding of their roles, responsibilities, and performance targets, as well as the support and resources they need to succeed. This, in turn, can help foster a culture of accountability, engagement, and collaboration, ultimately leading to improved performance and organizational success.

4.2 Monitoring and Measuring Performance

Effectively monitoring and measuring the performance of employees in hybrid and remote teams can be a complex process, but it is essential for maintaining a high level of productivity and engagement. This chapter will provide insights and best practices for monitoring and measuring performance in hybrid and remote teams, focusing on the following key areas: establishing performance metrics, leveraging technology for performance tracking, creating a culture of continuous improvement, and addressing performance issues proactively.

1. Establishing Performance Metrics

To effectively monitor and measure the performance of hybrid and remote employees, it is essential to establish clear performance metrics. These metrics should align with the organization's overall objectives and provide a quantifiable way to evaluate employee performance. Some examples of performance metrics include:

a. Task completion rates: The percentage of tasks or projects completed by an employee within a given timeframe.

b. Quality of work: The extent to which an employee's work meets or exceeds established quality standards.

c. Sales or revenue generation: The value of sales or revenue generated by an employee.

d. Customer satisfaction: The satisfaction levels of customers who interact with an employee or receive their services.

When establishing performance metrics, it is important to ensure that they are realistic, achievable, and tailored to the unique needs and circumstances of each employee. This may involve adjusting metrics based on an employee's specific skills, experience, or workload, as well as considering any external factors that may impact performance.

2. Leveraging Technology for Performance Tracking

With the advancements in technology, there are numerous tools available to help organizations monitor and measure the performance of hybrid and remote employees. These tools can provide real-time insights into employee performance, streamline the performance management process, and facilitate more accurate and objective evaluations. Some popular performance tracking tools include:

a. Time-tracking software: Allows employees to track the time they spend on specific tasks or projects, providing insights into productivity levels and areas for improvement.

b. Project management platforms: Facilitate collaboration and communication between team members and provide a centralized location to track project progress, deadlines, and performance metrics.

c. Performance management software: Offers features such as goal setting, performance tracking, and performance review management, streamlining the performance management process and providing a comprehensive overview of employee performance.

When implementing technology for performance tracking, it is important to consider factors such as ease of use, integration with existing systems, and scalability to ensure that the chosen tools are a good fit for the organization's needs and can support its growth over time.

3. Creating a Culture of Continuous Improvement

In addition to establishing performance metrics and leveraging technology for performance tracking, it is essential to create a culture of continuous improvement within the organization. This involves encouraging employees to regularly assess their performance, identify areas for growth or improvement, and actively work towards enhancing their skills and capabilities. Some strategies for fostering a culture of continuous improvement include:

a. Encouraging self-assessment: Provide employees with the tools and resources to regularly evaluate their performance, set personal goals, and track their progress towards achieving those goals.

b. Promoting learning and development: Offer opportunities for employees to expand their skills and knowledge, such as through training programs, mentorship, or professional development resources.

c. Recognizing and rewarding improvement: Acknowledge and celebrate employees who demonstrate significant growth or improvement in their performance, either through formal recognition programs or informal praise and encouragement.

4. Addressing Performance Issues Proactively

Despite the best efforts to monitor and measure performance, it is inevitable that some employees will face challenges or experience performance issues. It is essential to address these issues proactively and constructively, focusing on identifying the root cause of the issue and providing the necessary support and resources to help the employee improve. Some strategies for addressing performance issues include:

a. Regular check-ins: Schedule regular check-ins with employees to discuss their performance, address any concerns or challenges, and provide feedback and guidance.

b. Performance improvement plans: Develop a clear and actionable plan to help employees address performance issues, including specific goals, timelines, and resources or support.

c. Providing additional training and support: Offer targeted training or coaching to help employees address skill gaps or overcome obstacles that may be hindering their performance.

d. Re-evaluating workload and responsibilities: Assess whether an employee's workload or responsibilities may be contributing to performance issues and adjust as needed to ensure that they are set up for success.

e. Encouraging open communication: Foster a culture of open and honest communication, where employees feel comfortable discussing performance issues and seeking support or guidance from their manager or colleagues.

In conclusion, monitoring and measuring the performance of hybrid and remote employees is a critical component of effective performance management. By establishing clear performance metrics, leveraging technology for performance tracking, creating a culture of continuous improvement, and proactively addressing performance issues, organizations can ensure that their hybrid and remote teams remain engaged, productive, and aligned with the organization's overall objectives.

4.3: Feedback and Performance Reviews

Feedback and performance reviews play a vital role in the development and success of employees, particularly in hybrid and remote work environments. Providing constructive feedback and conducting regular performance reviews can help maintain alignment, identify areas for improvement, and reinforce positive behaviours. This chapter will explore the importance of feedback and performance reviews for hybrid and remote teams, different types of feedback, and best practices for conducting effective performance reviews.

Importance of Feedback and Performance Reviews for Hybrid and Remote Teams

In a hybrid or remote work setting, employees may have limited face-to-face interaction with their colleagues and supervisors. Consequently, it is crucial to prioritize feedback and performance reviews to ensure that employees feel connected and engaged. Regular feedback and performance reviews can:

1. Enhance employee engagement: Regular feedback can help employees feel more connected to their team and organization, fostering a sense of belonging and improving overall engagement.

2. Identify areas for improvement: Performance reviews can help identify skill gaps, areas for growth, and opportunities for professional development.

3. Reinforce positive behaviours: Providing constructive feedback can help reinforce positive behaviours and encourage employees to continue demonstrating high performance.

4. Promote accountability: Regular performance reviews can help hold employees accountable for their performance and ensure alignment with organizational goals and objectives.

5. Support employee growth and development: Feedback and performance reviews can provide employees with valuable insights into their strengths and weaknesses, helping them grow professionally and personally.

Types of Feedback

Effective feedback can take many forms, including:

1. Informal feedback: This type of feedback is often given in real-time, during day-to-day interactions between colleagues or supervisors and employees. Informal feedback can be a powerful tool for reinforcing positive behaviours or quickly addressing performance issues.

2. Formal feedback: Formal feedback typically occurs during scheduled performance reviews or evaluations. This type of feedback is more structured and often includes specific metrics and goals.

3. Positive feedback: Positive feedback acknowledges and reinforces an employee's achievements and accomplishments, helping to build their confidence and motivation.

4. Constructive feedback: Constructive feedback focuses on areas for improvement and provides actionable suggestions to help employees grow and develop their skills.

5. Peer feedback: Peer feedback allows employees to receive input from their colleagues, which can provide valuable insights and promote a culture of collaboration and continuous improvement.

Best Practices for Conducting Effective Performance Reviews

To ensure that performance reviews are effective and impactful, consider the following best practices:

1. Set clear expectations: Clearly communicate the purpose, format, and expectations for the performance review. Make sure employees understand the goals of the review process and how their performance will be assessed.

2. Use objective criteria: Develop objective criteria and metrics for evaluating employee performance, such as key performance indicators (KPIs) or quantifiable goals. This can help ensure a fair and consistent review process.

3. Encourage self-assessment: Encourage employees to conduct a self-assessment of their performance prior to the review. This can help employees reflect on their accomplishments and areas for improvement, facilitating a more productive and meaningful discussion.

4. Foster a two-way dialogue: Performance reviews should be a collaborative and open conversation between the employee and their supervisor. Encourage employees to share their thoughts, concerns, and ideas during the review process.

5. Focus on growth and development: Frame performance reviews as an opportunity for growth and development, rather than simply an evaluation of past performance. Discuss opportunities for professional development, such as training, mentorship, or new projects, and create a plan for improvement.

6. Provide specific and actionable feedback: Ensure that feedback is specific, actionable, and tied to concrete examples. This can help employees better understand their strengths and weaknesses and make meaningful improvements.

7. Follow up on action items: After the performance review, establish a timeline for implementing any agreed-upon action items or improvements. Regularly follow up with employees to ensure they are making progress and provide additional support as needed.

8. Encourage ongoing feedback: Promote a culture of continuous feedback and improvement by encouraging employees and supervisors to engage in regular, informal feedback conversations outside of formal performance reviews.

9. Adapt to individual needs: Recognize that employees have different preferences and needs when it comes to feedback and performance reviews. Some may prefer more frequent check-ins, while others may need more detailed feedback. Tailor your approach to each employee's unique needs and preferences to maximize the impact of performance reviews.

10. Leverage technology: Utilize technology, such as performance management software, to streamline the review process, track progress, and facilitate ongoing communication between employees and supervisors.

11. Train managers and supervisors: Ensure that managers and supervisors are equipped with the skills and knowledge needed to provide effective feedback and conduct meaningful performance reviews. Provide training and resources to help them develop strong coaching and communication skills.

12. Evaluate the performance review process: Regularly assess the effectiveness of your organization's performance review process and adjust as needed. Solicit feedback from employees and supervisors to identify areas for improvement and implement changes accordingly.

Feedback and performance reviews are essential components of performance management in hybrid and remote teams. By prioritizing regular feedback and implementing best practices for conducting performance reviews, organizations can support employee growth and development, reinforce positive behaviours, and ensure alignment with organizational goals and objectives. As the world continues to evolve and hybrid and remote work become more commonplace, investing in effective feedback and performance review practices will become increasingly critical to maintaining a productive and engaged workforce.

Chapter 5: Employee Engagement and Well-being – Introduction

In today's rapidly changing work environment, with the increasing prevalence of hybrid and remote work models, employee engagement and well-being have emerged as critical factors that can significantly impact the overall success of an organization. Engaged, motivated, and mentally healthy employees are more likely to be productive, innovative, and committed to their work, which in turn contributes to the organization's growth and sustainability. In contrast, disengaged employees or those struggling with their well-being can lead to decreased productivity, higher turnover rates, and a negative impact on the organization's culture and morale.

This chapter will delve into the importance of employee engagement and well-being in hybrid and remote teams and provide practical strategies for fostering a sense of belonging, encouraging work-life balance, and supporting mental health and well-being in the context of remote work. By focusing on these key aspects, organizations can ensure that their employees remain engaged and well-supported, irrespective of where they are working.

Section 5.1, "Fostering a Sense of Belonging," will explore the concept of belonging and its significance in remote work environments. This section will provide insights into how organizations can create a culture of inclusivity and connectedness that helps employees feel valued, heard, and supported, even when working remotely.

In section 5.2, "Encouraging Work-Life Balance," we will discuss the importance of maintaining a healthy balance between work and personal life in the context of remote work. This section will offer practical tips for organizations to support their employees in managing their workload, setting boundaries, and ensuring that they have ample time to recharge and maintain their overall well-being.

Finally, section 5.3, "Supporting Mental Health and Well-being," will address the crucial issue of mental health and its impact on employee engagement and performance. This section will outline strategies that organizations can adopt to promote mental health awareness, provide support to employees experiencing mental health challenges, and foster a psychologically safe work environment that enables employees to thrive.

By implementing the strategies outlined in this chapter, organizations can ensure that their hybrid and remote employees remain engaged, motivated, and well-supported, thereby maximizing their potential and driving the organization's success in the long run.

5.1: Fostering a Sense of Belonging

A sense of belonging plays a crucial role in employee engagement, motivation, and overall satisfaction. When employees feel connected to their team and organization, they are more likely to be productive, proactive, and committed to their work. In the context of hybrid and remote teams, fostering a sense of belonging can be challenging due to the physical distance and varying work schedules among team members. This section will explore strategies and best practices for nurturing a sense of belonging in hybrid and remote teams.

1. Create an inclusive and diverse culture: Inclusivity and diversity are the foundations of a strong sense of belonging. Encourage open communication, respect for individual differences, and appreciation for diverse perspectives. This can be achieved by implementing diversity and inclusion training, celebrating cultural events, and promoting a zero-tolerance policy for discrimination.

2. Establish regular check-ins and team meetings: Frequent communication is essential in building a sense of connectedness among team members. Schedule regular check-ins and team meetings to provide opportunities for team members to collaborate, share updates, and discuss any challenges they might be facing. These meetings should be inclusive and designed to accommodate team members working in different time zones.

3. Encourage team-building activities: Virtual team-building activities can help foster camaraderie and a sense of belonging among remote team members. Organize events such as virtual coffee breaks, online games, or team challenges to facilitate informal interactions and bonding among team members.

4. Provide opportunities for personal growth and development: Supporting employee growth and development contributes to a sense of belonging by demonstrating the organization's commitment to their well-being and success. Offer training, mentorship programs, and opportunities for skill development to help employees grow both personally and professionally.

5. Develop a buddy system: Pairing new employees with experienced team members can help newcomers feel welcomed and supported, facilitating a smoother onboarding process. The buddy system enables new employees to ask questions, seek guidance, and build relationships with their colleagues.

6. Recognize and celebrate achievements: Acknowledging employees' accomplishments and milestones can significantly impact their sense of belonging and motivation. Implement a recognition program that highlights individual and team achievements and celebrates work anniversaries, promotions, and personal milestones.

7. Encourage cross-functional collaboration: Encouraging employees to collaborate across departments and functions can help break down silos and create a sense of unity among team

members. Establish cross-functional projects or initiatives that provide employees with opportunities to work together, share ideas, and learn from each other.

8. Promote psychological safety: Creating a psychologically safe environment where employees feel comfortable sharing their thoughts, ideas, and concerns is essential in fostering a sense of belonging. Encourage open communication, listen actively, and demonstrate empathy and understanding when addressing employees' concerns.

9. Facilitate a virtual watercooler: Informal conversations and casual interactions are vital in building relationships and fostering a sense of belonging among team members. Create a dedicated virtual space, such as a chat room or discussion board, where employees can engage in non-work-related conversations, share personal interests, and get to know each other on a more personal level.

10. Offer support for remote work challenges: Remote employees may face unique challenges such as feelings of isolation, difficulty setting boundaries, and managing work-life balance. Providing support and resources to address these challenges can help remote employees feel understood and valued.

11. Encourage employee feedback and suggestions: Inviting employees to share their feedback and ideas on how to improve the workplace and team dynamics can contribute to a sense of belonging and ownership. Regularly solicit feedback and involve employees in the decision-making process when implementing changes.

12. Communicate organizational values and mission: Emphasizing the organization's values, mission, and goals can help employees feel connected to the organization's larger purpose and foster a sense of belonging. Regularly communicate and reinforce the organization's values, mission, and objectives, and highlight how each employee's work contributes to achieving these goals.

13. Develop a supportive leadership style: Leaders play a crucial role in fostering a sense of belonging among their team members. Adopt a supportive and empathetic leadership style that focuses on understanding employees' needs, providing guidance, and offering encouragement. Leaders should be approachable, open to feedback, and dedicated to the well-being and success of their team members.

14. Facilitate work-life balance: Encouraging and supporting work-life balance is essential for employees' mental and emotional well-being. Provide resources and flexibility to help employees manage their personal and professional lives effectively. This might include offering flexible work hours, promoting the importance of taking breaks, and providing mental health resources.

15. Create a sense of shared identity: Cultivating a shared identity among team members can contribute to a stronger sense of belonging. Develop a team mission statement, slogan, or set of shared values that can serve as a unifying force for the group. Encourage team members to identify with and take pride in these shared aspects of their team culture.

16. Be intentional about onboarding and offboarding: A well-structured onboarding process can help new employees feel welcomed and integrated into the team from the beginning. Similarly, thoughtful offboarding practices can help departing employees feel valued and supported in their transition. Ensure that both processes are designed with a focus on creating a positive and inclusive experience.

In conclusion, fostering a sense of belonging is essential for the success and well-being of employees in hybrid and remote teams. By implementing the strategies and best practices outlined in this section, organizations can create an inclusive and supportive environment that encourages employees to feel connected, valued, and engaged. A strong sense of belonging not only contributes to higher levels of employee satisfaction and motivation but also supports the overall success and growth of the organization.

5.2: Encouraging Work-Life Balance

In today's fast-paced and connected world, striking a healthy work-life balance is more important than ever. For hybrid and remote teams, achieving this balance can be particularly challenging due to the blurring of lines between personal and professional spaces. However, fostering a work-life balance is crucial for maintaining employee well-being, reducing stress, and promoting long-term engagement and productivity. In this section, we will explore various strategies and best practices to help organizations encourage work-life balance among their hybrid and remote employees.

1. Establish clear boundaries: One of the most significant challenges for remote employees is setting and maintaining boundaries between their work and personal lives. Encourage employees to establish and adhere to a regular work schedule, create a dedicated workspace, and avoid working during their personal time. Managers should lead by example, setting expectations for when they will be available and respecting employees' personal time.

2. Implement flexible work hours: Flexible work arrangements can play a significant role in helping employees achieve a better work-life balance. By allowing employees to work during the hours that best suit their personal and family needs, organizations can empower them to manage their professional and personal responsibilities more effectively.

3. Encourage time off: Encourage employees to take breaks, vacations, and personal days to recharge and avoid burnout. Managers should actively promote a culture that values time off and discourages the "always-on" mentality. Organizations can also consider implementing policies such as mandatory vacation days or "no-meeting" days to further emphasize the importance of downtime.

4. Support parental and family leave: Family and parental leave policies play a vital role in helping employees achieve work-life balance, particularly during significant life events such as the birth or adoption of a child or caring for an aging parent. Ensure that your organization's policies are supportive and flexible, allowing employees the necessary time to focus on their family needs.

5. Offer resources for stress management: Stress management is an essential aspect of achieving work-life balance. Provide employees with access to resources, such as stress management workshops, mindfulness training, or employee assistance programs, to help them manage stress and maintain their well-being.

6. Provide opportunities for personal development: Encouraging personal development can contribute to a better work-life balance by helping employees feel more fulfilled and satisfied in their lives outside of work. Offer resources and opportunities for personal development, such as online courses, workshops, or mentorship programs, to support employees in their personal growth.

7. Encourage regular breaks and physical activity: Taking regular breaks and engaging in physical activity can help employees maintain their well-being and achieve a better work-life balance. Encourage employees to take short breaks throughout the day, go for a walk, or engage in other forms of physical activity to maintain their energy levels and mental clarity.

8. Foster a culture of open communication: Open communication is critical in addressing and resolving work-life balance issues. Encourage employees to discuss their challenges and needs openly with their managers and colleagues and provide channels for anonymous feedback. Managers should be attentive and responsive to employee concerns, and work together with their team members to find solutions that support a healthy work-life balance.

9. Prioritize and delegate effectively: Encourage employees to prioritize their tasks and delegate when appropriate. This can help reduce the pressure to work long hours and enable employees to focus on their most important and meaningful work. Managers should also ensure that workloads are distributed equitably across the team and provide support and resources to help employees manage their tasks effectively.

10. Measure and monitor work-life balance: Regularly assess employee satisfaction and well-being and identify areas where improvements can be made to support work-life balance. This can be done through surveys, one-on-one meetings, or other feedback mechanisms. Use the insights gathered to inform organizational policies and practices and drive continuous improvement in fostering a healthy work-life balance for employees.

11. Celebrate achievements and personal milestones: Recognizing and celebrating employees' achievements and personal milestones can help create a positive work environment and contribute to a better work-life balance. Managers should take the time to acknowledge employees' accomplishments, both professionally and personally, and encourage team members to do the same. This can help strengthen relationships within the team and reinforce the importance of maintaining a healthy balance between work and personal life.

12. Model healthy work-life balance from the top: Senior leaders and managers play a critical role in setting the tone for work-life balance within an organization. By modelling healthy behaviours, such as taking time off, setting boundaries, and engaging in self-care, leaders can demonstrate their commitment to work-life balance and inspire their teams to follow suit.

13. Provide opportunities for team building and social connection: Building strong relationships among team members can contribute to a better work-life balance by fostering a supportive and collaborative work environment. Organize regular team-building activities and opportunities for social connection, such as virtual coffee breaks, team lunches, or after-work social events, to help employees build connections and feel more engaged with their colleagues.

14. Encourage employee autonomy: Empowering employees to take ownership of their work and make decisions about how they manage their time can contribute to a better work-life balance. Encourage employees to set their own goals, prioritize tasks, and determine the most effective ways to complete their work. This sense of autonomy can help employees feel more in control of their work-life balance and better equipped to manage their professional and personal responsibilities.

15. Continuously evaluate and adjust: Work-life balance is not a one-size-fits-all concept, and what works for one employee may not work for another. Regularly evaluate and adjust your organization's approach to work-life balance, considering individual employee needs, preferences, and circumstances. This ongoing process of evaluation and adjustment will help ensure that your organization remains responsive and supportive of employees' work-life balance needs.

In conclusion, fostering a healthy work-life balance is essential for employee well-being, engagement, and productivity. By implementing the strategies and best practices outlined in this chapter, organizations can help their hybrid and remote employees achieve a better balance between their professional and personal lives, ultimately benefiting both the individual and the organization as a whole.

5.3: Supporting Mental Health and Well-being

The mental health and well-being of employees are crucial to their overall engagement, productivity, and job satisfaction. With the rise of hybrid and fully remote teams, organizations need to take proactive measures to support the mental health of their employees, who may face unique challenges related to remote work, such as isolation, burnout, and difficulties in setting boundaries between work and personal life. This chapter will outline strategies and best practices for organizations to foster a mentally healthy work environment and support the well-being of their hybrid and remote employees.

1. Develop a comprehensive mental health policy: Establishing a mental health policy can serve as the foundation for promoting employee well-being and addressing mental health challenges in the workplace. The policy should outline the organization's commitment to fostering a mentally healthy work environment, its approach to supporting employees experiencing mental health challenges, and the resources available to employees for seeking help and support.

2. Promote awareness and understanding of mental health: Combat the stigma surrounding mental health by providing education and resources to help employees understand the importance of mental well-being and recognize the signs of mental health challenges. Offer training sessions, workshops, and webinars on topics related to mental health, stress management, and self-care, and provide easily accessible resources and materials for employees to reference at their convenience.

3. Encourage open dialogue and communication: Foster a culture of openness and support by encouraging employees to discuss mental health challenges and share their experiences. Managers should create a safe environment for these conversations by actively listening, showing empathy, and providing non-judgmental support. Regular check-ins between managers and employees can help identify potential mental health challenges and provide an opportunity to discuss strategies for addressing them.

4. Provide access to mental health resources and support: Ensure that employees have access to professional mental health support, such as Employee Assistance Programs (EAPs) or mental health professionals, as well as self-help resources and tools. These resources should be easily accessible and communicated regularly to employees, so they are aware of the available support options.

5. Implement flexible work arrangements: Offering employees flexibility in their work schedules and arrangements can help alleviate some of the stress and pressures associated with balancing work and personal life. By providing options such as flexible working hours, compressed workweeks, or job sharing, employees can better manage their mental well-being and find a healthier balance between their professional and personal responsibilities.

6. Encourage regular breaks and time off: Employees should be encouraged to take regular breaks throughout the day to recharge and manage stress. Additionally, organizations should emphasize the importance of taking time off, including vacations and mental health days, to help employees maintain their mental well-being and prevent burnout.

7. Foster social connections and peer support: Building strong social connections and support networks can be an essential factor in maintaining employees' mental health and well-being. Encourage team members to connect with one another through both formal and informal channels, such as virtual coffee breaks, team lunches, or after-work social events. Additionally, consider implementing a peer support program, where employees can connect with colleagues who have faced similar challenges and can offer guidance and support.

8. Provide manager training and support: Managers play a crucial role in supporting employees' mental health and well-being. Provide training and resources for managers to help them recognize the signs of mental health challenges, foster open dialogue and communication, and offer appropriate

support and resources to their team members. Encourage managers to regularly check in with their employees and address any concerns or challenges related to mental health and well-being.

9. Establish a culture of recognition and appreciation: Recognizing and appreciating employees' hard work and accomplishments can contribute to a positive work environment and support employees' mental health and well-being. Develop a culture of recognition and appreciation through both formal and informal channels, such as regular feedback, team meetings, or company-wide recognition programs. Make sure to acknowledge not only employees' professional achievements but also their efforts in supporting their colleagues' mental well-being and fostering a positive work environment.

10. Monitor and address workplace stressors: Identify common workplace stressors that may negatively impact employees' mental health and well-being, such as excessive workload, unrealistic expectations, or lack of autonomy. Implement strategies to address these stressors and create a more supportive work environment. Regularly solicit feedback from employees to identify new stressors and adjust policies and practices accordingly.

11. Offer stress-reduction and self-care initiatives: Encourage employees to engage in stress-reduction activities and prioritize self-care as part of their daily routines. Offer resources and programs that promote relaxation and stress management, such as meditation, yoga, or mindfulness workshops. Encourage employees to take regular breaks and engage in physical activity or hobbies that help them recharge and maintain their mental well-being.

12. Measure the effectiveness of mental health and well-being initiatives: Regularly assess the effectiveness of your organization's mental health and well-being initiatives by collecting data on employee satisfaction, engagement, and mental health outcomes. Use this information to identify areas for improvement and refine your organization's approach to supporting employee mental health and well-being.

By implementing these strategies and best practices, organizations can create a supportive and mentally healthy work environment for their hybrid and remote employees. Supporting employees' mental health and well-being not only benefits the individual but also contributes to the overall success of the organization by fostering a more engaged, productive, and satisfied workforce. As remote and hybrid work arrangements continue to evolve, it is crucial for organizations to prioritize mental health and well-being as a key component of their employee engagement and support strategies.

Chapter 6: Real-Life Examples of Successful Hybrid and Remote Organizations

In previous chapters, we have discussed the fundamentals of hybrid and remote work, organizational structures, communication and collaboration, performance management, and employee engagement and well-being in the context of hybrid and remote teams. As organizations continue to navigate the complexities of remote work and adapt their strategies to better suit the evolving workplace landscape, it is beneficial to examine real-life examples of organizations that have successfully implemented hybrid and remote work models. By exploring the experiences of these companies, we can identify best practices, learn from their successes and challenges, and draw valuable insights for our own organizations.

In this chapter, we will delve into the stories of three successful hybrid and remote organizations: GitLab, Buffer, and Automattic. These companies have not only embraced remote work but also thrive in the remote environment by prioritizing transparency, trust, flexibility, and decentralization in their organizational culture and practices. Each company offers a unique perspective on hybrid and remote work, providing insights into different approaches and strategies that have led to their success.

First, we will explore GitLab, a company known for its pioneering approach to remote work and its commitment to transparency and asynchronous communication. GitLab's remote-first culture and extensive documentation practices enable employees to collaborate effectively across time zones and geographical boundaries. We will examine how GitLab's dedication to transparency and asynchronous communication has contributed to its success as a remote organization.

Next, we will investigate Buffer, a company that has built a culture of trust and flexibility around its remote work model. Buffer's emphasis on employee autonomy, transparency, and continuous learning has created an environment where employees feel empowered to make decisions, take risks, and develop their skills. We will discuss how Buffer's focus on trust and flexibility has driven its growth as a remote company.

Finally, we will examine Automattic, the company behind WordPress.com, and its unique approach to decentralizing decision-making within its remote workforce. Automattic's flat organizational structure and distributed decision-making processes promote collaboration, innovation, and employee engagement. We will explore how Automattic's commitment to decentralization has facilitated its success as a remote organization.

By studying these real-life examples, we can gain a deeper understanding of the strategies and best practices that have enabled these organizations to excel in the remote work environment. These insights can inform our own approaches to hybrid and remote work, helping us develop more effective organizational structures, communication frameworks, and employee support systems to ensure the success and well-being of our remote and hybrid teams.

6.1: GitLab: Embracing Transparency and Async Communication

GitLab, a leading provider of web-based Git repository management, has become one of the most successful remote organizations in the world. With a team of over 1,000 employees spread across more than 65 countries, GitLab has managed to build a strong, inclusive, and productive remote work culture. One of the key factors behind GitLab's success in remote work is its unwavering commitment to transparency and asynchronous communication.

Transparency at GitLab

Transparency is at the core of GitLab's culture and business model. The company believes that by fostering a transparent work environment, it can create a sense of trust and ownership among employees, leading to greater collaboration, innovation, and efficiency. To promote transparency, GitLab has implemented several strategies:

1. Open-source mindset: GitLab's roots are in the open-source community, and the company has embraced the open-source mentality of sharing knowledge and collaborating with others. GitLab's product is available in both free and paid versions, with the free version offering most features to the public. This open-source mindset extends to GitLab's internal processes, with employees encouraged to share their knowledge and collaborate across teams.

2. Public handbook: GitLab's handbook is a comprehensive guide to the company's culture, processes, and guidelines, and is publicly available online. By making the handbook accessible to everyone, GitLab ensures that employees, customers, and

the wider community can understand the company's values, operations, and decision-making processes. The handbook is continuously updated by employees, with over 3,000 pages of information, reflecting the collective knowledge and expertise of the entire organization.

3. Open meetings and documentation: GitLab holds many of its meetings and discussions openly, allowing employees from different teams and departments to join and contribute their insights. Meeting agendas, notes, and recordings are often shared internally, promoting a culture of information sharing and collaboration. Additionally, GitLab encourages employees to document their work, processes, and decisions, so that their knowledge can be easily accessed and built upon by others.

Asynchronous Communication

As a global company with employees in different time zones, GitLab relies heavily on asynchronous communication to ensure that everyone can collaborate effectively and efficiently. Asynchronous communication refers to communication that does not happen in real-time, allowing individuals to respond to messages and requests at their own pace. GitLab has implemented several practices to support asynchronous communication:

1. Preference for written communication: GitLab emphasizes written communication, as it allows employees to communicate their thoughts and ideas clearly and can be easily referenced and shared. Employees are encouraged to provide context and details when sharing information, and to avoid relying solely on synchronous tools like video calls and instant messaging. This preference for written communication ensures that information is accessible and understandable to all employees, regardless of their location and working hours.

2. Utilizing collaboration tools: GitLab leverages a variety of tools to support asynchronous collaboration, including GitLab Issues, Merge Requests, and Google Docs. These tools enable employees to work on projects, provide feedback, and make decisions together, without the need for constant real-time communication. By using these tools, employees can contribute to projects when it suits their schedule, reducing the pressure to be constantly online and responsive.

3. Encouraging time zone flexibility: GitLab acknowledges that working across time zones can be challenging and encourages employees to be flexible in their working hours to accommodate collaboration with colleagues in various locations. Employees are not expected to be available 24/7 but are encouraged to find a balance that allows them to collaborate effectively while maintaining a healthy work-life balance.

Benefits of GitLab's Approach

GitLab's commitment to transparency and asynchronous communication has resulted in several benefits for the organization:

1. Enhanced collaboration and innovation: By fostering an environment of openness and trust, GitLab employees feel empowered to share ideas, ask questions, and collaborate across teams and departments. This collaborative atmosphere drives innovation, as employees can build on each other's expertise and work together to create innovative solutions and improvements.

2. Greater efficiency and productivity: By embracing asynchronous communication, GitLab allows employees to work at their own pace and manage their time more effectively. This

leads to increased efficiency, as employees can focus on their most important tasks without constant interruptions from real-time communication. Additionally, the emphasis on written communication and documentation ensures that information is easily accessible, reducing the need for repetitive meetings and discussions.

3. Improved employee satisfaction and retention: GitLab's transparent and flexible work culture contributes to higher levels of employee satisfaction and engagement. Employees feel a sense of ownership and responsibility, knowing that their contributions are valued, and their voices are heard. This supportive environment, combined with the flexibility to work from anywhere and manage their own schedules, leads to better work-life balance and increased retention of top talent.

4. Stronger company reputation: GitLab's commitment to transparency has earned the company a reputation as a thought leader in the remote workspace. By sharing its internal processes, culture, and learnings with the public, GitLab has positioned itself as a trusted resource for other organizations looking to adopt remote work practices. This powerful reputation has led to increased brand recognition and customer trust, ultimately contributing to GitLab's business success.

Lessons for Other Organizations

GitLab's success in embracing transparency and asynchronous communication offers valuable insights for other organizations looking to implement remote work:

1. Prioritize transparency: Encourage openness and trust within your organization by sharing information, involving employees in decision-making processes, and creating a culture of shared knowledge and collaboration.

2. Emphasize written communication: Focus on clear and detailed written communication to ensure that information is easily accessible and understandable for all employees, regardless of their location and working hours.

3. Leverage technology for asynchronous collaboration: Utilize collaboration tools that support asynchronous communication, allowing employees to work together and contribute to projects without the need for constant real-time interaction.

4. Be flexible and accommodating: Recognize the challenges of working across time zones and encourage employees to find a balance between collaborating with colleagues and maintaining a healthy work-life balance.

By adopting these practices, organizations can successfully implement remote work models, leading to greater collaboration, efficiency, and employee satisfaction. GitLab's experience demonstrates that a commitment to transparency and asynchronous communication can drive success in the remote work era, creating a resilient and innovative organization ready to face the challenges of the future.

6.2: Buffer- Building a Culture of Trust and Flexibility

Buffer is a social media management company that has successfully built a fully remote work culture, embracing trust, flexibility, and transparency. With employees working across multiple time zones, Buffer has developed a unique approach to managing remote work, emphasizing employee autonomy, well-being, and communication. This chapter will explore the key elements of Buffer's remote work culture and discuss the lessons other organizations can learn from their success.

Key Elements of Buffer's Remote Work Culture

1. Emphasizing trust and autonomy: Buffer operates on the principle that employees should be trusted to manage their own work and schedules. Instead of micromanaging or imposing strict working hours, the company encourages employees to take ownership of their tasks and work in a way that suits them best. This approach fosters a sense of trust and autonomy, empowering employees to be more productive and engaged.

2. Focusing on results, not hours: Rather than monitoring the number of hours employees work, Buffer evaluates performance based on results and outcomes. This outcome-oriented approach allows employees to focus on the quality of their work, rather than the time spent completing tasks. By emphasizing results, Buffer ensures that employees are held accountable for their performance, while still providing the flexibility to manage their own schedules.

3. Encouraging work-life balance: Buffer recognizes the importance of maintaining a healthy work-life balance, especially in a remote work environment. The company actively promotes self-care and encourages employees to take time off when needed, including offering unlimited vacation days. Buffer also provides resources and support for employee well-being, such as mental health support and virtual team-building activities.

4. Transparent communication: Buffer is committed to open and transparent communication, both internally and externally. The company shares ts business strategies, financial information, and even employee salaries with the public, fostering a culture of openness and accountability. Within the organization, Buffer encourages open communication through regular check-ins, virtual meetings, and collaboration tools, ensuring that employees stay connected and informed.

5. Continuous learning and development: Buffer invests in the personal and professional development of its employees, offering resources and opportunities for growth. The company provides a personal development fund for each employee to use for courses, conferences, or other learning experiences. Buffer also encourages employees to share their knowledge and skills with one another, fostering a culture of continuous learning and improvement.

Impact of Buffer's Remote Work Culture

Buffer's unique remote work culture has led to numerous benefits for both the company and its employees:

1. Increased employee engagement and satisfaction: By fostering a culture of trust and autonomy, Buffer has seen increased levels of employee engagement and satisfaction. Employees feel empowered to take ownership of their work, leading to higher levels of motivation and productivity.

2. Attraction and retention of top talent: Buffer's remote work culture and emphasis on work-life balance have made the company an attractive employer, allowing it to attract and retain top talent from around the world. By offering flexibility and support, Buffer has been able to build a diverse and skilled workforce that contributes to the company's success.

3. Enhanced innovation and creativity: Buffer's culture of continuous learning and open communication encourages employees to share ideas, collaborate, and think creatively. This environment fosters innovation, as employees can build on one another's expertise and develop innovative solutions to challenges.

4. Strong company reputation: Buffer's commitment to transparency and employee well-being has earned the company a formidable reputation in the remote work community. This reputation has led to increased brand recognition and customer trust, ultimately contributing to Buffer's business success.

Lessons for Other Organizations

Buffer's success in building a culture of trust and flexibility offers valuable insights for other organizations looking to implement remote work:

1. Trust employees to manage their own work: Encourage autonomy and trust by allowing employees to manage their own schedules and workloads. This approach not only empowers employees but also leads to increased productivity and engagement.

2. Focus on results, not hours: Evaluate employee performance based on outcomes, rather than the number of hours worked. This shift in focus enables employees to prioritize the quality of their work and ensures accountability without compromising flexibility.

3. Prioritize work-life balance and well-being: Promote a healthy work-life balance by providing support and resources for employee well-being. Encourage time off, offer mental health support, and facilitate team-building activities to maintain a strong remote work culture.

4. Communicate openly and transparently: Foster a culture of open communication and transparency by sharing company information and encouraging regular check-ins and virtual meetings. This approach keeps employees connected and informed, while also building trust and accountability.

5. Invest in employee development: Support continuous learning and development by providing resources and opportunities for growth. Encourage knowledge-sharing and collaboration to create a culture of continuous improvement.

6. Be adaptable and open to change: Remote work is an evolving landscape, and organizations must be willing to adapt and embrace change. Learn from successful remote companies like Buffer and be open to experimenting with novel approaches to remote work.

In conclusion, Buffer's remote work culture demonstrates the power of trust, flexibility, and transparency in creating a successful and engaged workforce. By prioritizing employee autonomy, work-life balance, and open communication, Buffer has built a strong remote work culture that contributes to the company's success. Organizations looking to implement remote work can learn valuable lessons from Buffer's approach and adapt these principles to their own unique contexts.

6.3: Automattic: Decentralizing Decision-Making

Automattic, the company behind WordPress.com, WooCommerce, Tumblr, and other well-known web services, has been a pioneer in remote work since its founding in 2005. With more than 1,500 employees spread across 80 countries, Automattic has not only thrived in a fully remote environment but also serves as a role model for other organizations seeking to adopt remote work practices. In this chapter, we will explore Automattic's approach to decentralizing decision-making and the impact this has on their organizational success.

1. Flat organizational structure

Automattic's organizational structure is unique in that it is intentionally flat, with very few levels of hierarchy. This flat structure fosters a culture of empowerment and autonomy, where employees are encouraged to take responsibility for their own decisions and actions. The company's founder, Matt Mullenweg, believes that this structure enables employees to be more creative and collaborative, as they are not bogged down by bureaucracy or traditional top-down management.

2. Empowering teams with autonomy

At Automattic, each team is given a high level of autonomy in deciding how they work and what projects they focus on. This autonomy allows teams to adapt quickly to new challenges and opportunities, while also ensuring that they are constantly learning and growing. Teams are also encouraged to experiment with new tools and processes to find the best ways of working together, which contributes to the company's culture of continuous improvement.

3. Distributed decision-making

In line with their flat organizational structure, Automattic practices distributed decision-making, where employees are trusted to make decisions without always seeking approval from higher-ups. This approach not only speeds up the decision-making process but also fosters a sense of ownership and accountability among employees. By empowering employees to make decisions, Automattic creates an environment where individuals are more likely to feel engaged and committed to their work.

4. Open and transparent communication

Automattic prioritizes open and transparent communication, which is essential for a decentralized decision-making process. The company utilizes various communication tools and practices, such as P2 (a WordPress-based internal communication platform) and regular video conferences, to keep employees informed and connected. This open communication ensures that employees have access to the information they need to make informed decisions and collaborate effectively.

5. Cross-functional collaboration

Automattic encourages cross-functional collaboration by organizing employees into small, multidisciplinary teams, known as "squads." These squads work together on specific projects or initiatives, allowing employees with different skills and expertise to collaborate and learn from one another. This collaborative approach fosters innovation and helps to break down silos within the organization.

6. Continuous learning and development

A commitment to continuous learning and development is a key aspect of Automattic's decentralized decision-making process. The company offers a range of learning opportunities, such as internal workshops, online courses, and an annual professional development budget for each employee. By investing in employee development, Automattic ensures that its workforce is equipped with the skills and knowledge needed to make informed decisions and contribute to the company's success.

7. Trust and accountability

For a decentralized decision-making process to be successful, trust and accountability are critical. Automattic fosters a culture of trust by giving employees the freedom and autonomy to make decisions, while also holding them accountable for the outcomes of those decisions. This balance of trust and accountability ensures that employees are motivated to make the best decisions for the company and their teams.

8. Embracing change and innovation

Automattic's decentralized decision-making process also enables the company to be more agile and responsive to change. By empowering employees to make decisions and experiment with innovative ideas, Automattic can quickly adapt to recent technologies and market trends. This adapts ability has allowed the company to remain at the forefront of the ever-evolving digital landscape and maintain a competitive edge in their industry.

9. Measuring success and iterating

To ensure the effectiveness of their decentralized decision-making process, Automattic continuously measures and evaluates the success of their teams and projects. By collecting data and feedback, the company can identify areas for improvement and adjust as needed. This iterative approach ensures that the decision-making process remains effective and continues to support the company's growth and development.

10. Lessons for other organizations

Automattic's success in implementing a decentralized decision-making process offers valuable insights for other organizations considering a shift to remote or hybrid work models. Some key takeaways include:

- Embrace a flat organizational structure to empower employees and reduce bureaucracy.

- Foster a culture of trust and accountability to support decentralized decision-making.

- Prioritize open and transparent communication to keep employees informed and engaged.

- Encourage cross-functional collaboration to drive innovation and break down silos.

- Invest in continuous learning and development to equip employees with the skills and knowledge needed to make informed decisions.

- Be agile and responsive to change, embracing innovative technologies and market trends.

- Measure success and iterate to ensure the effectiveness of the decision-making process.

In conclusion, Automattic's approach to decentralizing decision-making has played a crucial role in their success as a fully remote organization. By empowering employees, fostering a culture of trust and accountability, and prioritizing open communication and collaboration, Automattic has created an environment where individuals can thrive and contribute to the company's continued growth. By adopting these principles and practices, other organizations can also benefit from the advantages of decentralized decision-making and build successful remote or hybrid teams.

Chapter 7: Implementing Change: A Step-by-Step Guide

Transitioning to a hybrid or fully remote work model can be a significant change for any organization. To ensure a smooth and successful transition, it is essential to follow a structured approach that addresses the various aspects of remote work, from organizational structure and communication to performance management and employee well-being. This chapter aims to provide a comprehensive step-by-step guide for organizations looking to implement a hybrid or fully remote work model, drawing on the best practices and lessons learned from successful remote organizations.

The process of implementing a remote work model should be approached with a strategic mindset, considering the unique needs and characteristics of your organization. It is essential to consider the different factors that can impact the success of remote work, such as organizational culture, technology, and employee preferences. By carefully planning and executing each step of the implementation process, organizations can minimize potential challenges and maximize the benefits of remote work.

The first step in implementing a remote work model is assessing your organization's readiness for change. This involves evaluating the current state of your organization, identifying potential barriers to remote work, and understanding the needs and preferences of your employees. This assessment will provide valuable insights into the changes that need to be made and help you develop a sharp vision for your organization's future.

Once you have assessed your organization's readiness, the next step is to develop a remote work policy that outlines the guidelines and expectations for employees working remotely. This policy should address topics such as communication, technology, performance management, and employee well-being, ensuring that employees have a clear understanding of what is expected of them in a remote work environment.

With a remote work policy in place, the next step is to revisit roles and responsibilities within your organization. This may involve restructuring teams, redefining job descriptions, or introducing new roles to support remote work. It is essential to ensure that employees have the necessary support and resources to succeed in their roles, whether they are working remotely or in the office.

Pilot testing is a crucial step in the implementation process, allowing organizations to test their remote work model on a small scale before rolling it out more broadly. This provides an opportunity to identify any issues or challenges and adjust as needed, ensuring that the remote work model is effective and sustainable for the long term.

Finally, monitoring and continuous improvement are essential for maintaining the success of your remote work model. By regularly reviewing your remote work practices and gathering feedback from employees, you can identify areas for improvement and make ongoing adjustments to ensure that your organization continues to thrive in a remote or hybrid work environment.

In this chapter, we will delve deeper into each of these steps, providing practical advice and guidance for organizations looking to implement a successful hybrid or fully remote work model. By following this step-by-step guide, you can confidently navigate the transition to remote work and create a positive and productive work environment for your employees.

7.1: Assessing Your Organization's Readiness

Before implementing a hybrid or fully remote work model, it is crucial to assess your organization's readiness for this significant change. This process involves evaluating several factors, including your current infrastructure, organizational culture, employee preferences, and potential barriers to remote work. By conducting a thorough assessment, you can identify the necessary adjustments and develop a roadmap for a successful transition. This chapter will discuss the key areas to consider when assessing your organization's readiness for remote work.

1. Infrastructure and Technology

The foundation of any successful remote work model is a robust technological infrastructure that supports seamless communication and collaboration among employees. Evaluate your current infrastructure and identify any gaps or limitations that need to be addressed. Consider the following:

- Internet connectivity: Ensure that employees have access to stable and high-speed internet connections, both at the office and at their remote work locations.

- Hardware and software: Assess whether employees have the necessary hardware (e.g., laptops, monitors, headsets) and software (e.g., project management tools, video conferencing platforms) to work effectively in a remote environment.

- Security and data protection: Evaluate your organization's data security measures and policies, ensuring that remote employees can access and share information securely.

2. Organizational Culture

A supportive organizational culture is vital for the success of remote work. Assess your current culture to identify any potential barriers to remote work and determine how your organization can foster a remote-friendly environment. Key aspects to consider include:

- Trust and autonomy: Gauge the level of trust between managers and employees and whether team members are comfortable working independently.

- Communication: Assess the effectiveness of your current communication practices and identify any areas for improvement, such as promoting openness and transparency.

- Collaboration: Evaluate how well your teams collaborate and share knowledge, both within and across departments.

3. Employee Preferences and Skills

Understanding employee preferences and skills is essential for developing a remote work model that meets their needs and supports their professional growth. Conduct surveys or interviews to gather insights into the following:

- Employee preferences: Determine the proportion of employees who prefer to work remotely, in the office, or in a hybrid arrangement. Identify their preferred work schedules and any specific needs or challenges they may face in a remote setting.

- Skillsets: Assess employees' existing skills and identify any gaps that may need to be addressed through training or development programs. Consider both technical skills (e.g., using remote collaboration tools) and soft skills (e.g., self-management, communication).

4. Managerial Support

Managers play a crucial role in facilitating the success of remote work arrangements. Assess their readiness to support remote employees and identify any areas for development. Consider the following:

- Management styles: Evaluate whether managers have experience managing remote employees and whether their management styles align with the needs of remote workers, such as promoting autonomy and trust.

- Training and development: Identify any training or development needs for managers, such as coaching on effective remote management practices or providing resources to help them support their teams.

5. Legal and Regulatory Considerations

Before implementing a remote work model, it is essential to understand and comply with any legal and regulatory requirements that may apply. Consult with legal and HR experts to ensure that your organization is prepared to address the following:

- Employment laws and regulations: Review applicable employment laws and regulations, such as working hours, overtime, and employee classification, to ensure compliance in a remote work context.

- Tax and payroll implications: Understand the tax and payroll implications of remote work, particularly if employees will be working from different states or countries.

- Data privacy and security: Ensure that your organization complies with any relevant data privacy and security regulations, such as the General Data Protection Regulation (GDPR) or the California Consumer Privacy Act (CCPA).

6. Financial Impact

Assess the budgetary impact of implementing a hybrid or remote work model to ensure that it aligns with your organization's financial goals and resources. Consider both the short-term and long-term implications, including:

- Cost savings: Evaluate potential cost savings from reducing office space, utilities, and other overhead expenses. This will help you understand how remote work can contribute to your organization's financial objectives.

- Investment in technology and infrastructure: Estimate the cost of investing in the necessary technology and infrastructure upgrades to support remote work, including hardware, software, and network upgrades.

- Employee compensation and benefits: Assess the potential impact of remote work on employee compensation and benefits, such as adjustments to salaries based on geographic location or offering stipends for home office setups.

- Training and development costs: Estimate the cost of providing training and development programs for employees and managers to support the transition to remote work.

7. Identifying Potential Roadblocks

As part of your readiness assessment, it is essential to identify any potential roadblocks that may hinder the successful implementation of a hybrid or remote work model. These roadblocks could include:

- Resistance to change: Understand the concerns and objections of employees or managers who may be resistant to the idea of remote work. Address these concerns by providing clear communication, education, and support throughout the transition.

- Technical challenges: Identify any technical challenges that may arise during the implementation process, such as integrating new software or troubleshooting connectivity issues, and develop a plan to address them.

- Cultural barriers: Recognize any cultural barriers that may impede the adoption of remote work, such as a strong attachment to traditional office-based work or a lack of trust in remote employees. Develop strategies to overcome these barriers by promoting a remote-friendly culture and addressing any misconceptions about remote work.

By thoroughly assessing your organization's readiness for hybrid or remote work, you can develop a comprehensive plan to address any gaps or challenges and lay the foundation for a successful transition. This assessment will help you make informed decisions and ensure that your organization is well-prepared to embrace the future of work.

7.2. Developing a Remote Work Policy

A well-crafted remote work policy is crucial for the successful implementation of a hybrid or remote work model. It provides a clear framework for both employees and managers, addressing expectations, responsibilities, and guidelines that help create a productive and inclusive remote work environment. This section outlines the key elements to include in your remote work policy and how to create a policy that reflects your organization's unique needs and values.

1. Establish Eligibility Criteria

Determine which positions or roles within your organization are suitable for remote work. Consider factors such as the nature of the job, the level of interaction with clients or colleagues, and access to necessary resources or equipment. Clearly outline the eligibility criteria in your remote work policy to ensure transparency and fairness.

2. Define Remote Work Arrangements

Remote work arrangements can vary significantly, from fully remote positions to flexible hybrid models that combine in-office and remote work. Specify the distinct types of remote work arrangements available within your organization, including any restrictions or conditions that apply to each. For example, you may require employees to work a certain number of days in the office or have a trial period before transitioning to a more permanent remote arrangement.

3. Set Expectations for Availability and Communication

Outline the expectations for employee availability and communication while working remotely. This may include core working hours during which employees are expected to be online and responsive, as well as any specific communication tools or platforms they should use. Emphasize the importance of maintaining open lines of communication and staying connected with colleagues and supervisors.

4. Establish Performance Metrics and Goals

Remote work requires a shift in focus from time spent in the office to measurable outcomes and results. Clearly define the performance metrics and goals that remote employees will be evaluated on, ensuring that they align with your organization's broader objectives. This will help maintain accountability and encourage a results-driven remote work culture.

5. Address Technology and Equipment Needs

Identify the technology and equipment required to support remote work, including hardware, software, and network access. Specify who is responsible for providing these resources and any associated costs, as well as guidelines for the appropriate use of company-owned devices and software. Additionally, outline any security protocols or best practices that remote employees should follow to protect sensitive information and maintain data privacy.

6. Create Guidelines for Health and Safety

Remote employees may face unique health and safety challenges, such as maintaining a proper ergonomic workstation or managing work-related stress. Develop guidelines that address these issues and promote a healthy remote work environment. This may include recommendations for ergonomic equipment, tips for maintaining work-life balance, and resources for mental health support.

7. Outline the Approval Process

Describe the process for requesting and approving remote work arrangements, including any required documentation or forms. Identify the individuals or departments responsible for reviewing and approving these requests, as well as any applicable deadlines or waiting periods.

8. Implement a Review and Adjustment Period

Remote work policies should be adaptable and responsive to the evolving needs of your organization and its employees. Establish a review and adjustment period, during which you will evaluate the effectiveness of your remote work policy and make any necessary updates or changes. This could include gathering feedback from employees and managers, analysing performance data, or conducting surveys to identify areas for improvement.

9. Develop an Onboarding and Training Program

Ensure that new and existing employees are prepared for remote work by developing a comprehensive onboarding and training program. This should cover topics such as remote work best practices, using communication and collaboration tools, and understanding the expectations outlined in your remote work policy.

10. Communicate the Remote Work Policy

Once your remote work policy is developed, communicate it clearly and consistently throughout your organization. Make the policy easily accessible to all employees and provide opportunities for questions and clarification. Regularly revisit and reinforce the policy to ensure that employees remain informed and engaged with the expectations and guidelines.

11. Promote a Culture of Trust and Accountability

A successful remote work policy is built on a foundation of trust and accountability. Encourage managers to trust their remote employees, empowering them to make decisions and manage their time effectively. Similarly, remote employees should understand their responsibility to maintain open communication and deliver results in line with organizational goals. Foster a culture where trust and accountability are valued and reinforced through regular communication, feedback, and recognition.

12. Address Legal and Compliance Issues

When developing your remote work policy, be sure to consider any legal and compliance issues that may arise. This may include labour laws, tax implications, and data protection regulations that apply to remote employees, particularly those working in different states or countries. Consult with legal and HR professionals to ensure your policy adheres to all applicable laws and regulations.

13. Provide Ongoing Support and Resources

Remote work can present unique challenges and opportunities for employees. Offer ongoing support and resources to help them navigate these challenges and maximize their potential. This may include access to professional development programs, mentorship opportunities, or mental health resources. Regularly check in with remote employees to ensure they have the support they need to be successful in their roles.

14. Foster Inclusivity and Employee Engagement

An effective remote work policy should promote inclusivity and engagement for all employees, regardless of their work arrangements. This includes providing equal opportunities for professional growth, ensuring that remote employees are included in team meetings and events, and promoting a sense of belonging and connection. Foster a culture where remote employees feel valued and supported, and their contributions are recognized and celebrated.

15. Continuously Evaluate and Improve Your Remote Work Policy

The success of your remote work policy will depend on your ability to continuously evaluate and improve upon it. Regularly gather feedback from employees and managers, analyse performance data, and stay informed about best practices and emerging trends in remote work. Use this information to make data-driven decisions and refine your policy over time, ensuring it remains relevant and effective in supporting your organization's goals and objectives.

In conclusion, developing a comprehensive and well-thought-out remote work policy is a critical step in implementing a successful hybrid or fully remote work model. By addressing key elements such as eligibility, communication, performance metrics, technology, health and safety, and fostering trust and accountability, your organization can create a remote work environment that supports employee engagement, productivity, and well-being. As remote work continues to evolve, remain adaptable and responsive to the changing needs of your organization and employees, ensuring your remote work policy remains an effective tool for success.

7.3. Revisiting Roles and Responsibilities

In the process of implementing a hybrid or fully remote work model, it is crucial to revisit the roles and responsibilities within your organization. Ensuring that employees have clearly defined roles and expectations can significantly impact the success of your remote work model. This chapter will provide guidance on redefining roles and responsibilities in a remote work context, including the importance of alignment, fostering autonomy, and supporting collaboration among team members.

1. Alignment with Organizational Goals and Objectives

Start by revisiting your organization's goals and objectives to ensure that roles and responsibilities remain aligned with your overall strategy. Evaluate how each role contributes to the achievement of these goals and identify any adjustments needed to accommodate the new remote work model. This may involve restructuring teams or departments, modifying job descriptions, or even creating entirely new roles.

2. Clarity and Specificity

In a remote work environment, it is essential to provide clear and specific expectations for each role. This includes outlining the key responsibilities, performance metrics, and deliverables associated with each position. Consider using a role-based competency framework to define the skills, knowledge, and behaviours required for success in each role. Providing employees with detailed job descriptions and performance expectations can help mitigate confusion, ensure accountability, and support a sense of purpose and direction.

3. Autonomy and Decision-Making

Remote work often necessitates a higher level of autonomy and decision-making ability among employees. As you revisit roles and responsibilities, consider how to empower employees to make decisions and manage their work independently. This may involve delegating authority, providing employees with the resources and tools necessary for success, or implementing a more flexible management style that supports employee autonomy.

4. Collaboration and Teamwork

While autonomy is essential in a remote work environment, so too is collaboration and teamwork. Ensure that roles and responsibilities within your organization are structured in a way that promotes collaboration and the effective sharing of information. This may involve creating cross-functional teams, implementing team-based goals, or establishing communication protocols that facilitate collaboration.

5. Support and Resources

As roles and responsibilities shift in a remote work context, it is crucial to provide employees with the support and resources necessary for success. This may include training and development opportunities, access to remote work tools and technology, or mentorship and guidance from managers or colleagues. Ensure that employees are well-equipped to navigate their new responsibilities and that they have the support they need to excel in their roles.

6. Flexibility and Adaptability

Remote work requires a high level of flexibility and adaptability, both from employees and the organization as a whole. As you revisit roles and responsibilities, consider how to build flexibility into your organization's structure. This may involve implementing agile methodologies, allowing for role rotation, or embracing a growth mindset that encourages continuous learning and adaptation.

7. Inclusivity and Equity

As you redefine roles and responsibilities, it is essential to ensure that your organization remains inclusive and equitable for all employees, regardless of their work location or arrangements. This includes providing equal opportunities for professional growth, ensuring remote employees are included in team meetings and events, and promoting a sense of belonging and connection. Foster a culture where remote employees feel valued and supported, and their contributions are recognized and celebrated.

8. Continuous Improvement and Feedback

Lastly, revisit roles and responsibilities regularly to ensure they remain relevant and effective in supporting your organization's goals and objectives. Gather feedback from employees and managers, analyse performance data, and stay informed about best practices and emerging trends in remote work. Use this information to make data-driven decisions and refine your organizational structure over time, ensuring it remains agile and responsive to the changing needs of your organization and employees.

In conclusion, revisiting roles and responsibilities is a critical step in successfully implementing a hybrid or fully remote work model. By ensuring that roles are aligned with organizational goals, providing clarity and specificity, fostering autonomy and collaboration, offering support and resources, and prioritizing flexibility, inclusivity, and continuous improvement, your organization will be well-positioned for success in a remote work environment.

Remember that the transition to a remote or hybrid work model is an ongoing process that requires adaptability, communication, and a commitment to learning from both successes and challenges. Continuously engaging with your employees and refining your approach will help create a more resilient and effective organization, capable of thriving in an increasingly digital and remote world.

As you move forward with implementing change, keep in mind that the goal is to create a work environment that supports employee productivity, well-being, and engagement, while also driving organizational growth and success. By thoughtfully revisiting roles and responsibilities, you will be better equipped to navigate the complexities of remote work and ultimately create a more dynamic, collaborative, and successful organization.

7.4. Pilot Testing and Iteration

Before fully implementing a remote or hybrid work model across your organization, it is crucial to conduct pilot tests to identify potential issues, gather feedback, and refine your approach. Pilot testing offers valuable insights into the feasibility and effectiveness of your remote work policy, communication strategies, and support systems. In this chapter, we will explore the importance of pilot testing and iteration and provide guidance on designing and executing successful pilot programs.

1. Identifying the scope and objectives of the pilot test

Start by defining the scope and objectives of your pilot test. Determine which departments, teams, or employees will be involved, and establish clear goals for the test. This could include assessing the effectiveness of communication tools, measuring productivity, evaluating employee satisfaction, or identifying any technical or logistical challenges that may arise in a remote work environment. By setting specific, measurable, achievable, relevant, and time-bound (SMART) objectives, you can better evaluate the success of your pilot test and make informed decisions about implementing remote work on a broader scale.

2. Selecting participants and establishing a timeline

Carefully select the participants for your pilot test, ensuring they represent a diverse cross-section of your organization. This might include employees with varying levels of seniority, job functions, and experience with remote work. Be sure to communicate the purpose, expectations, and timeline for the pilot test clearly to all participants. Establish a realistic timeline for the test, allowing sufficient time to identify and address any challenges, gather feedback, and refine your approach as needed.

3. Monitoring progress and gathering feedback

Throughout the pilot test, closely monitor the progress of participating employees, teams, and departments. Keep track of any challenges, successes, or unexpected outcomes that arise during the test. Regularly gather feedback from participants, using a combination of surveys, one-on-one meetings, and group discussions. Encourage open and honest communication and provide participants with a safe space to share their experiences, concerns, and suggestions.

4. Analysing results and identifying areas for improvement

Once the pilot test has concluded, thoroughly analyse the results to determine the success of your remote work policy, communication strategies, and support systems. Identify any areas where improvements are needed, and use the feedback gathered from participants to inform your decisions. If the pilot test highlights significant challenges or gaps in your remote work policy, consider revisiting earlier stages of the process, such as assessing your organization's readiness or refining your remote work policy.

5. Iterating and refining your approach

Based on the findings of your pilot test, make any necessary adjustments to your remote work policy, communication strategies, and support systems. This might involve refining your expectations around communication and collaboration, implementing innovative technology solutions, or providing additional resources and training for employees. As you iterate and refine your approach, continue to gather feedback from employees and stakeholders to ensure your remote work policy remains effective and aligned with the needs of your organization.

6. Expanding the pilot test or implementing organization-wide

After iterating and refining your approach, consider expanding the pilot test to include additional departments, teams, or employees. This will provide further opportunities to identify potential challenges, gather feedback, and refine your remote work policy. Once you are confident that your remote work policy is effective and scalable, begin implementing it across your organization.

7. Continuously evaluating and adapting

The process of implementing and refining a remote work policy is ongoing. Regularly evaluate the effectiveness of your remote work policy, communication strategies, and support systems, and be prepared to adjust as needed. This might involve reassessing the needs of your employees, staying informed about advancements in remote work technology, or refining your approach to employee engagement and well-being. By continuously evaluating and adapting, you can ensure your organization remains agile and responsive in an ever-evolving remote work landscape.

7.5. Monitoring and Continuous Improvement

To maintain the success of your remote or hybrid work model, it is essential to regularly monitor performance and engagement while continually improving your policies and practices. In this chapter, we will explore the importance of monitoring and continuous improvement and provide guidance on maintaining the effectiveness of your remote work policy over time.

1. Establishing key performance indicators (KPIs)

Begin by identifying the key performance indicators (KPIs) that will help you measure the success of your remote work policy. These KPIs might include productivity metrics, employee engagement and satisfaction levels, retention rates, and the quality of work produced. Be sure to align your KPIs with your organization's overall goals and objectives to ensure that your remote work policy contributes to the success of your business.

2. Conducting regular evaluations

Regular evaluations are crucial for monitoring the effectiveness of your remote work policy and identifying areas for improvement. Conduct evaluations on a consistent basis, such as quarterly or annually, to track your organization's progress and make data-driven decisions. Include employee surveys, performance reviews, and feedback sessions as part of your evaluation process to gather insights from various sources.

3. Analysing data and identifying trends

After collecting data through evaluations, analyse the results to identify trends and patterns that may indicate the strengths and weaknesses of your remote work policy. Look for correlations between specific policies or practices and your KPIs and use this information to inform your continuous improvement efforts. Be open to adapting your approach based on the data and feedback you receive.

4. Encouraging a culture of continuous improvement

Fostering a culture of continuous improvement within your organization is essential for maintaining the success of your remote work policy. Encourage employees to embrace a growth mindset and view change as an opportunity for growth rather than a threat. Provide resources and training to help employees develop the skills they need to thrive in a remote or hybrid work environment and create open channels for communication and feedback so employees can share their ideas and concerns.

5. Iterating and refining your remote work policy

Based on the insights gained from your evaluations and data analysis, make any necessary adjustments to your remote work policy. This might involve updating your communication guidelines, implementing recent technology solutions, or providing additional support for employee well-being. Continually refine your policy to better meet the needs of your organization and employees and be prepared to make changes as the remote work landscape evolves.

6. Sharing best practices and lessons learned

Encourage collaboration and knowledge sharing within your organization by openly discussing the best practices and lessons learned from your remote work policy implementation. Hold regular meetings or workshops where employees can share their experiences, ask questions, and offer suggestions for improvement. This collective approach can help your organization identify new strategies and techniques for enhancing the remote work experience.

7. Monitoring external developments and industry trends

Stay informed about the latest developments in remote work, including innovative technology solutions, research findings, and industry trends. Regularly assess how these developments may impact your organization and consider adjusting your remote work policy accordingly. This proactive approach will help you stay ahead of the curve and ensure that your organization remains competitive in a rapidly changing business landscape.

8. Celebrating successes and acknowledging challenges

As you work toward continuous improvement, it is essential to recognize and celebrate the successes of your remote work policy. Share positive stories and achievements with your team and acknowledge the hard work and dedication that has contributed to these successes. At the same time, openly address any challenges or setbacks that have arisen, and use these experiences as learning opportunities to drive further improvements.

9. Revisiting your remote work policy

Regularly revisit your remote work policy to ensure that it remains up-to-date and aligned with your organization's goals and objectives. As your business grows and evolves, you may need to adjust your policy to accommodate new team members, shifting priorities, or changes in the remote work landscape. By proactively reviewing and updating your policy, you can maintain its effectiveness and support the long-term success of your remote or hybrid work model.

10. Investing in technology and infrastructure

To sustain the success of your remote work policy, invest in technology and infrastructure that supports seamless communication, collaboration, and productivity. Continuously evaluate the tools and platforms used by your organization to ensure they meet the needs of your remote and hybrid workforce. Stay abreast of emerging technologies and consider incorporating them into your tech stack to further enhance the remote work experience for your employees.

11. Focusing on employee well-being

Employee well-being is a critical component of a successful remote work policy. Regularly assess the well-being of your remote and hybrid employees by monitoring engagement, satisfaction, and mental health indicators. Provide resources, training, and support to help employees maintain a healthy work-life balance and be proactive in addressing any well-being concerns that arise.

12. Soliciting and implementing feedback

Employee feedback is invaluable for the continuous improvement of your remote work policy. Encourage employees to share their thoughts, concerns, and suggestions through a variety of channels, such as surveys, one-on-one meetings, and group discussions. Actively listen to their feedback and be willing to adjust based on their input. This open communication will help build trust and ensure that your remote work policy remains responsive to the needs of your workforce.

In conclusion, monitoring and continuous improvement are essential for maintaining the success of your remote or hybrid work model. By regularly evaluating your policy, analysing data, and iterating based on feedback, you can ensure that your remote work policy remains effective and sustainable over time. Embrace a culture of continuous improvement and be prepared to adapt as the remote work landscape evolves to keep your organization competitive and agile.

Epilogue:

Throughout this guide, we have explored the intricacies of hybrid and fully remote teams, discussing their benefits, challenges, and the factors that influence their organizational design. As a first step, readers can identify quick wins and long-term investments that will contribute to the successful implementation of a remote or hybrid work model.

A quick win that can be immediately applied is the establishment of a robust communication framework. Begin by setting clear communication guidelines and expectations, selecting the right tools for effective collaboration, and promoting a culture of openness and transparency. This foundation will not only facilitate remote work but also improve overall team dynamics and productivity.

Another area for immediate improvement is performance management. Ensure that expectations and goals are well-defined and communicated to all team members. By fostering a sense of accountability and ownership, organizations can optimize team performance in a remote or hybrid setting.

In the long term, organizations should invest in designing an effective organizational structure that supports remote work and encourages agility. This includes transitioning from traditional structures to more flexible and adaptive models. Although this transformation may require significant effort, the resulting increase in responsiveness and adaptability will prove invaluable in an ever-changing business landscape.

Employee engagement and well-being are essential components of a successful remote or hybrid work model, necessitating long-term investment. Start by fostering a sense of belonging among team members and encouraging a healthy work-life balance. Over time, these efforts will translate into increased job satisfaction, higher retention rates, and improved overall performance.

Looking at the real-life examples of GitLab, Buffer, and Automattic, organizations can learn valuable lessons from their successful implementation of remote and hybrid work models. These companies have embraced transparency, trust, flexibility, and decentralized decision-making as key components of their organizational culture.

The step-by-step guide provided in this resource outlines the process of implementing change in your organization. Start by assessing your organization's readiness for remote work, develop a remote work policy, and revisit roles and responsibilities. Following this, conduct pilot testing and iteration, and continuously monitor and improve your remote work strategies.

In conclusion, transitioning to a remote or hybrid work model is a journey that requires ongoing commitment and learning. By focusing on quick wins and long-term investments, organizations can successfully adapt to the future of work. Embrace change, stay agile, and continuously seek improvement to unlock the full potential of remote work and ensure your organization's success in an ever-evolving business landscape.

References and Sources

1. Allen, T. D., Golden, T. D., & Shockley, K. M. (2015). How effective is telecommuting? Assessing the status of our scientific findings. Psychological Science in the Public Interest, 16(2), 40-68.

2. Choudhury, P., Foroughi, C., & Larson, B. Z. (2020). Work-from-anywhere: The productivity effects of geographic flexibility. Strategic Management Journal, 42(4), 655-683.

3. Duxbury, L. E., & Halinski, M. (2014). When more is less: An examination of the relationship between hours in telework and role overload. Work, 48(1), 91-103.

4. Gajendran, R. S., Harrison, D. A., & Delaney-Klinger, K. (2015). Are telecommuters remotely good citizens? Unpacking telecommuting's effects on performance via ideals and job resources. Personnel Psychology, 68(2), 353-393.

5. Hackman, J. R., & Oldham, G. R. (1975). Development of the job diagnostic survey. Journal of Applied Psychology, 60(2), 159-170.

6. Lister, K., & Harnish, T. (2011). The State of Telework in the U.S: How Individuals, Business, and Government Benefit. Telework Research Network.

7. Mael, F., & Ashforth, B. E. (1992). Alumni and their alma mater: A partial test of the reformulated model of organizational identification. Journal of Organizational Behavior, 13(2), 103-123.

8. Moe, N. B., & Šmite, D. (2008). Understanding a lack of trust in global software teams: A multiple-case study. Software Process: Improvement and Practice, 13(6), 511-526.

9. Nilles, J. M. (1998). Managing Telework: Strategies for Managing the Virtual Workforce. John Wiley & Sons.

10. Ployhart, R. E., & Vandenberg, R. J. (2010). Longitudinal research: The theory, design, and analysis of change. Journal of Management, 36(1), 94-120.

11. Van Dyne, L., Kossek, E. E., & Lobel, S. A. (2007). Less need to be there: Cross-level effects of work practices that support work-life flexibility and enhance group processes and group-level OCB. Human Relations, 60(8), 1123-1154.

12. Bloom, N., Liang, J., Roberts, J., & Ying, Z. J. (2015). Does working from home work? Evidence from a Chinese experiment. The Quarterly Journal of Economics, 130(1), 165-218.

13. DeFilippis, E., Impink, S. M., Singell, M., Polzer, J. T., & Sadun, R. (2020). Collaborating during coronavirus: The impact of COVID-19 on the nature of work. National Bureau of Economic Research Working Paper No. 27612.

14. Gallup. (2020). State of the American Workplace.

15. Harford, T. (2017). A world without work is coming – it could be utopia or it could be hell. The Guardian.

16. Marlow, S. L., Lacerenza, C. N., & Salas, E. (2017). Communication in virtual teams: a conceptual framework and research agenda. Human Resource Management Review, 27(4), 575-589.

17. Mesmer-Magnus, J. R., DeChurch, L. A., Jimenez-Rodriguez, M., Wildman, J., & Shuffler, M. (2011). A meta-analytic investigation of virtuality and information sharing in teams. Organizational Behavior and Human Decision Processes, 115(2), 214-225.

18. Morgan, J. (2020). The Future of Work: Attract New Talent, Build Better Leaders, and Create a Competitive Organization. John Wiley & Sons.

19. Sahinidis, A. G., & Bouris, J. (2008). Employee perceived training effectiveness relationship to employee attitudes. Journal of European Industrial Training, 32(1), 63-76.

20. World Health Organization. (2010). Telework and Health. Copenhagen: WHO Regional Office for Europe.

21. Zigurs, I., & Buckland, B. K. (1998). A theory of task/technology fit and group support systems effectiveness. MIS Quarterly, 22(3), 313-334.

22. Allen, N. J., & Meyer, J. P. (1990). The measurement and antecedents of affective, continuance and normative commitment to the organization. Journal of Occupational Psychology, 63(1), 1-18.

23. Bailey, D. E., & Kurland, N. B. (2002). A review of telework research: findings, new directions, and lessons for the study of modern work. Journal of Organizational Behavior, 23(4), 383-400.

24. Bélanger, F., & Allport, C. D. (2008). Collaborative technologies in knowledge telework: an exploratory study. Information Systems Journal, 18(1), 101-121.

25. Gajendran, R. S., & Harrison, D. A. (2007). The good, the bad, and the unknown about telecommuting: meta-analysis of psychological mediators and individual consequences. Journal of Applied Psychology, 92(6), 1524-1541.

26. Gibson, C. B., & Cohen, S. G. (2003). Virtual teams that work: Creating conditions for virtual team effectiveness. John Wiley & Sons.

27. Golden, T. D., Veiga, J. F., & Simsek, Z. (2006). Telecommuting's differential impact on work-family conflict: is there no place like home? Journal of Applied Psychology, 91(6), 1340-1350.

28. Hertel, G., Geister, S., & Konradt, U. (2005). Managing virtual teams: a review of current empirical research. Human Resource Management Review, 15(1), 69-95.

29. Martins, L. L., Gilson, L. L., & Maynard, M. T. (2004). Virtual teams: what do we know and where do we go from here? Journal of Management, 30(6), 805-835.

30. Raghuram, S., Hill, N. S., Gibbs, J. L., & Maruping, L. M. (2019). Virtual work: Bridging research clusters. Academy of Management Annals, 13(1), 308-341.

31. Spector, P. E. (2019). Do not cross me: optimizing the use of cross-sectional designs. Journal of Business and Psychology, 34(2), 125-137.